Workout

Skills Review & Practice

Reading Grade 5

Triumph Learning®

Workout, Reading, Grade 5
264NA
ISBN-10: 1-60471-115-9
ISBN-13: 978-1-60471-115-8

Cover Image: © Ralph Voltz/Deborah Wolfe Ltd.; © Rubberball/Jupiterimages;
© Imagesource/Photolibrary; © Creatas/Photolibrary.

Triumph Learning® 136 Madison Avenue, 7th Floor, New York, NY 10016
Kevin McAliley, President and Chief Executive Officer

Printed in the United States of America.

10 9 8 7 6 5

Dear Student,

Are you a reading champion?

You will be when you use

Workout!

Getting in shape is easy.

Just complete the lessons inside.

So, on your mark, get set – Work Out!

This book belongs to _____

Table of Contents

Unit 1: Reading for Information

Unit 2: Reading Literature

Unit 3: Editing

LESSON 1 — Context Clues

WORDS TO KNOW **Context clues** the words, phrases, or sentences around or near an unfamiliar word that help you understand its meaning

---

Review It! Read these sentences. Use the Hint to help you figure out the unfamiliar word.

A few weeks ago, Jihan got a new puppy. The puppy is not very obedient, so Jihan is taking him to a weekly dog-training class to teach him to do what he is told.

Hint Here, the phrase *do what he is told* helps you to understand what *obedient* means.

Try It! Read this passage. As you read, <u>underline</u> unfamiliar words and circle context clues that help you understand each word's meaning.

1 Long ago, the city of Tenochtitlán was the Aztec capital of the country now called
2 Mexico. It was built in the 1300s, and destroyed in 1521 by the Spanish army. The
3 Spanish were hungry for power and wanted to **control** Mexico. In order to do that,
4 they had to fight the Aztec people. The Aztec people were strong and the Spanish
5 army was small. But after the army blocked Tenochtitlán for almost three months,
6 the Spanish got control of the city. During the **siege**, no food or water came in and
7 no people were able to leave. Once the **ancient** city was overtaken and ruined, the
8 former capital became a **colony** ruled by Spain. The Spanish built a new city in the
9 same spot as the old one. Today, Mexico City sits on top of the ruins of Tenochtitlán.

Now, use the passage to answer the questions on the following page.

1. In line 3, the word "control" means to

    A. limit   C. destroy
    B. rule   D. rebuild

2. As used in line 6, "siege" **most likely** means a military operation in which

    A. a place is surrounded and outside supplies are cut off
    B. all of the buildings in a city are destroyed
    C. a large army comes in to defeat a weak enemy
    D. a colony is formed in the ruined location

Ask Yourself

2.
What phrase near the word *siege* in line 6 helps you figure out its meaning?

3. In line 7, the word "ancient" means

    A. strong
    B. large
    C. royal
    D. old

3.
If you replace *ancient* with each of these answer choices, which makes the most sense to you?

4. As used in line 8, "colony" **most likely** means a place that

    A. is ruled by the army
    B. has no capital city
    C. is ruled by a faraway country
    D. has a lot of supplies

In Your Own Words

5. Rewrite the last sentence of the passage in your own words.

    _____

    _____

    _____

    _____

5.
What does the word *ruins* mean to you?

On Your Own!   Read this passage. Answer the questions that follow it.

Salmon are amazing fish. For one thing, they can swim up river. Have you ever seen pictures of fish jumping out of a river as they fight and **struggle** to swim against fast-moving water? Those were probably salmon!

The female salmon lays as many as 10,000 eggs in gravel on the bottom of a river. After the eggs hatch, they grow to be about half an inch long. That's when they start swimming **downstream**, toward the salty ocean. As they travel, they eat and grow. Now they're called juvenile fish, which means they aren't babies anymore, but they aren't adults yet, either. Juvenile salmon can't survive in saltwater. Therefore, they spend about two years traveling in the **freshwater** of the river before making it all the way to the ocean. By the time they arrive, they're adults!

But only about 10 of those 10,000 eggs will have made it to **adulthood** and the open waters of the ocean. Those that do **survive** face new challenges in the dangerous ocean waters.

After living two to six years in the ocean, adult salmon are ready to **reproduce**, or have babies. This process is called **spawning**. The adult fish travel back to the same river in which they were born. This is the only place they will spawn! Adult males **frequently** die after spawning. They are very tired after traveling against the fast **current**. Female salmon are stronger, though. They live long enough to spawn three or four times in their life.

---

1. The word "struggle" means to

    A. try very hard

    B. calm down

    C. advance

    D. leap

2. Freshwater can be found in all of these bodies of water, except

    A. a lake

    B. a stream

    C. a pond

    D. an ocean

3. As used in the passage, "survive" means to

   A. die

   B. stay alive

   C. fight

   D. eat prey

4. As used in the passage, the word "current" means

   A. the flow of a stream

   B. a riverbed

   C. open ocean

   D. fish food

5. The word "frequently" means

   A. always

   B. never

   C. often

   D. rarely

6. Which phrase from the passage helps you figure out the meaning of "spawning"?

   A. "After living two to six years …"

   B. "…back to the same river…"

   C. "…ready to reproduce, or have babies."

   D. "…the only place they will spawn!"

Write It Out Write the meaning for each word from the passage in the space provided in the chart.

7.

Word	Meaning
freshwater	
downstream	
adulthood	
reproduce	

LESSON 2 Main Idea

WORDS TO KNOW | **Main idea** the most important idea of a passage, or what the passage is mostly about

---

Review It!

Read these sentences. Use the Hint to help you figure out the main idea.

Baking bread is no easy job. If a baker adds too much yeast, the bread will balloon to silly sizes. If the flour is packed too heavily, it won't rise properly. This is not an easy task!

Hint The first and last sentences both imply that baking bread is hard. This is what the paragraph is mostly about.

Try It!

Read this passage. <u>Underline</u> phrases and sentences that express the most important idea in the passage.

(1) Yo-Yo Ma is a famous musician. He plays the cello in concerts all over the world and has won awards for this talent. But what does he love as much as his cello? Education.

(2) Yo-Yo Ma was born in Paris in 1955. He and his parents later moved to New York. Yo-Yo Ma was five years old when he played in his first concert. He later went to Juilliard, a famous music school. But Mr. Ma wanted a well-rounded education, so he went on to study at Harvard University.

(3) Mr. Ma loves education as much as he loves music. He likes to teach children about music. One of the ways he has done this is through television. Yo-Yo Ma has been on the PBS shows *Sesame Street*, *Arthur*, and *Mister Rogers' Neighborhood*. In addition to appearing on children's shows, he has also visited many talk and news programs to share his ideas about music and education.

Now, use the passage to answer the questions on the following page.

1.   This passage is mainly about

   A. Yo-Yo Ma's music career

   B. how Yo-Yo Ma feels about music

   C. Yo-Yo Ma's education

   D. how important education is to Yo-Yo Ma

2.   Which sentence **best** states the main idea of this passage?

   A. Yo-Yo Ma values education.

   B. Yo-Yo Ma likes to be on television.

   C. Yo-Yo Ma was born in Paris.

   D. Yo-Yo Ma thinks music is important.

2.
Which of the answer choices are supporting details from the passage? These can't be the correct answer.

3.   Which of the following **best** states the main idea of paragraph 1?

   A. Yo-Yo Ma is a famous musician.

   B. Yo-Yo Ma performs around the world.

   C. Yo-Yo Ma has won awards for playing the cello.

   D. Yo-Yo Ma loves education as much as his cello.

3.
Which statement tells the most important idea from the paragraph? Some of the other statements may be true, but they don't tell what the paragraph is mostly about.

4.   What would make a good title for the entire passage?

   A. "Yo-Yo Ma and His Cello"

   B. "Yo-Yo Ma: A Man of Music and Education"

   C. "Yo-Yo Ma and His Television Appearances"

   D. "Yo-Yo Ma and His Children"

In Your Own Words

5.   Write a sentence that summarizes the entire passage.

_____

_____

_____

5.
What is this passage mostly about?

On Your Own!

Read this passage. Answer the questions that follow it.

Patricia MacLachlan has written a lot of books. Many of them, including *Sarah, Plain and Tall,* are about a family that lived in the vast American prairie lands at the turn of the century.

Ms. MacLachlan was born in Wyoming, and a lot of her books are about life on the farms and prairies of her birthplace. In her stories, Ms. MacLachlan brings back a way of life from the past. Her readers can almost feel the wind rush over the tall wheat and see the clouds in the endless sky.

Patricia MacLachlan has not lived in Wyoming in a long time. Now she lives in Massachusetts, where she has spent most of her life. Though there are no prairie lands there, Ms. MacLachlan remembers them well and re-creates them for her readers. She stays connected to Wyoming by carrying around a small bag filled with prairie soil.

Ms. MacLachlan does not depend on her birthplace as the only inspiration for her wonderful books. Her own children have inspired her as well, and she likes to use funny things they say as the beginning of books. But looking through the list of books Ms. MacLachlan has written, one can't help but notice a theme: frontier stories about life on the open farms and prairies of a time gone by.

1. This passage is mostly about

   A. a children's book writer
   B. a book series set in the past
   C. life on the prairie
   D. living in Massachusetts

2. What is the main idea of this passage?

   A. Patricia MacLachlan writes children's books.
   B. The American prairie inspired many of MacLachlan's books.
   C. Patricia MacLachlan writes books with her daughter.
   D. MacLachlan was born in Wyoming.

3. Which sentence **best** states the main idea of the second paragraph?

  A. Many of MacLachlan's books tell how life on the prairie used to be.

  B. MacLachlan was born in Wyoming, but she soon moved away.

  C. MacLachlan says the sky is bigger on the prairie.

  D. All of MacLachlan's books are about the old West.

4. Which paragraph is about MacLachlan re-creating Wyoming through her memory?

  A. first paragraph

  B. second paragraph

  C. third paragraph

  D. last paragraph

5. What is the last paragraph **mostly** about?

  A. MacLachlan's birthplace

  B. other things that inspire MacLachlan

  C. MacLachlan's children

  D. a book MacLachlan wrote about pets

6. A good title for this passage would be

  A. "An Award-Winning Writer"

  B. "The Life and Times of Patricia MacLachlan"

  C. "Patricia MacLachlan: An Author Inspired by Her Birthplace"

  D. "Prairies and Dogs: The Writing of Patricia MacLachlan"

Write It Out Use the passage to help you write a brief response to the prompt below.

7. Write the main idea of the passage in your own words.

_____

_____

_____

_____

3 Supporting Details

WORDS TO KNOW **Supporting details** the information that supports, or backs up, the main idea

---

Review It!

Read these sentences. Use the Hint to help you figure out the supporting details.

Whole-grain cereal makes a healthy morning meal. It gives you lots of energy. It contains many vitamins and has a lot of fiber. Pour in some calcium-packed milk, and you've got the perfect breakfast!

Hint The first sentence states the main idea. The other sentences back it up, or support it with facts and information.

Try It!

Read this passage. Underline phrases and sentences that support, or back up, the main idea of the passage.

(1) Lions are social animals known for their strength and beauty. They are very big cats that can weigh more than 500 pounds. They live in Africa in family groups called "prides."

(2) A pride of lions consists of one or two males and many more females and their cubs. The female lions hunt to feed the pride. They hunt in groups for zebras, antelope, and other animals. The males rarely hunt. They eat what the females bring back to the pride.

(3) Male lions are best known for their manes. People can often tell one lion apart from another because of their unique manes. The lion's mane has made him recognizable around the world.

(4) The majestic lion is a symbol of strength, leadership, and beauty in places very far away from his home in Africa.

Now, use the passage to answer the questions on the following page.

1. Which of these details from the passage is **not** an example of a supporting detail?

   A. "Lions are social animals known for their strength and beauty."

   B. "They live in Africa in family groups called 'prides.' "

   C. "They hunt in groups for zebras, antelope, and other animals."

   D. "The lion's mane has made him recognizable around the world."

1.
Which of the answer choices states the main idea of the passage? This must be the correct answer.

2. Who hunts to feed the lions in a pride?

   A. the males   C. the cubs

   B. the females   D. all of the members of the pride

3. According to the passage, what makes male lions recognizable all over the world?

   A. They can weigh up to 500 pounds.

   B. They eat zebras and antelope.

   C. They live in prides.

   D. Their manes are unique.

3.
Is there a keyword that appears in both the question and the passage?

4. According to the passage, a pride of lions is usually made up of

   A. many males, females, and cubs

   B. one or two males, many females, and cubs

   C. one male and several females

   D. one male, one female, and their cubs

In Your Own Words

5. Write down the main idea of the passage and three details that support it.

_____

_____

_____

5.
What details make lions different from other animals?

On Your Own!

Read this passage. Answer the questions that follow it.

Have you ever thought about where our food comes from? Foods are grown and produced all over the world. And many of those foods are shipped from far away to get to our kitchens. Almost all of the food in the grocery store travels hundreds of miles to get there. Most vegetables in our stores travel an average of 1,500 miles to get there. Nearly half of the fruit we eat is grown in other countries. Most of our red meat comes all the way from Australia and New Zealand. You can't travel much farther than that!

Shipping all that food can be bad for the environment. Why? Think about how food travels. It is trucked across highways in huge 18-wheelers. Or it's hauled in ships over oceans. Or it is flown around the world in airplanes. All of these vehicles burn a lot of fuel. Burning all that fuel pollutes the air. Air pollution can cause climate change, smog, and acid rain.

What can we do to help? One way is to buy local food. That means buying food that is grown or raised as close to home as possible. Imagine how much fuel we could save if we just stopped shipping food all over the world. Eating what grows locally could help save the planet!

---

1. What is the **best** title for this passage?

   A. "Eat Global, Buy Global"

   B. "Eat Locally to Save the Planet"

   C. "How Food Travels"

   D. "Red Meat around the World"

2. Which of these details **best** supports the main idea of the passage?

   A. Shipping food worldwide is good for businesses.

   B. Almost half the fruit we eat is grown in other countries.

   C. The vehicles that transport our food pollute the air.

   D. Some food is flown in airplanes to get to us.

3. Which is **not** a supporting detail from the first paragraph?

   A. Burning fuel pollutes the air and adds to climate change.

   B. Vegetables travel 1,500 miles to get to our country.

   C. Our red meat comes from Australia and New Zealand.

   D. Food in the grocery store travels hundreds of miles.

4. Which sentence from the passage backs up the idea that the transportation of food adds to air pollution?

   A. "Nearly half of the fruit we eat is grown in other countries."

   B. "Air pollution can cause climate change, smog, and acid rain."

   C. "That means buying food that is grown or raised as close to home as possible."

   D. "All of these vehicles burn a lot of fuel."

5. Which sentence from the passage does **not** support the idea that food travels a long way?

   A. "That means buying food that is grown or raised as close to home as possible."

   B. "Most vegetables in our stores travel an average of 1,500 miles to get there."

   C. "Almost all of the food in the grocery store travels hundreds of miles to get there."

   D. "Most of our red meat comes all the way from Australia and New Zealand."

6. Which detail from the passage would be most surprising if you knew that U.S. farmers grow a lot of broccoli?

   A. "Most of our red meat comes all the way from Australia and New Zealand."

   B. "Nearly half of the fruit we eat is grown in other countries."

   C. Most vegetables in our stores travel an average of 1,500 miles to get there.

   D. "Think about how food travels."

Write It Out Use the passage to help you write a brief response to the prompt below.

7. Write down the main idea of the second paragraph, and list three details that support it.

_____

_____

_____

LESSON 4 — Graphic Organizers

Graphic organizers visual aids that show information in an easy-to-read way. Tables, timelines, and bar graphs are examples.

Review It! Read this table. Use the Hint to help you figure out what information the table presents.

Student	Number of Raffle Tickets Sold
Mark	35
Juanita	48
Gabrielle	67

Hint The headings in the first row of the table explain what information is being presented. You know from reading them that students sold raffle tickets.

Try It! Read this bar graph. <u>Underline</u> the words that explain what information is being presented.

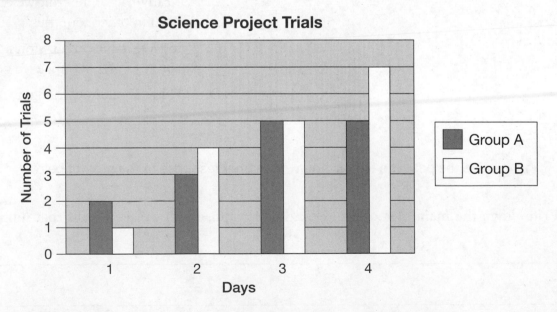

Science Project Trials

Now, use the bar graph to answer the questions on the following page.

1. On which day did the groups carry out the same number of trials?

   A. Day 1 **C.** Day 3

   B. Day 2 **D.** Day 4

2. On which day did Group B carry out the most trials?

   A. Day 1 **C.** Day 3

   B. Day 2 **D.** Day 4

3. On which day did Group A carry out the fewest trials?

   A. Day 1 **C.** Day 3

   B. Day 2 **D.** Day 4

4. Which sentence **best** describes the information presented in the bar graph?

   A. Two groups of students did a series of trials for their science project over the course of four days.

   B. Group A did the most trials for the science project.

   C. Four groups of students tried to make a science project work during one school week.

   D. Group B did the fewest trials on Day 1 of the science project.

In Your Own Words

5. Which group made the most progress over the course of the project? Explain your answer.

   _____

   _____

   _____

   _____

Ask Yourself

3.
Which color bar shows Group A? On which day is that color bar the shortest?

4.
Which two answer choices can you eliminate right away, knowing that they are too specific to answer this question?

5.
Does one color bar get longer over the course of the project than the other?

On Your Own!

Read this timeline. Answer the questions that follow it.

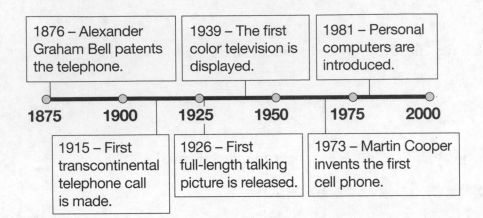

1876 – Alexander Graham Bell patents the telephone.

1939 – The first color television is displayed.

1981 – Personal computers are introduced.

1875   1900   1925   1950   1975   2000

1915 – First transcontinental telephone call is made.

1926 – First full-length talking picture is released.

1973 – Martin Cooper invents the first cell phone.

---

1. The timeline shows

   A. how science has advanced since 1950

   B. some important inventions in space exploration

   C. how scientists have worked together over the years

   D. some important inventions in technology

2. How many years does the timeline span?

   A. over 150 years

   B. over three centuries

   C. 125 years

   D. less than 100 years

3. How long after Alexander Graham Bell patented the telephone was the first transcontinental phone call made?

   A. 39 years later

   B. 37 years later

   C. 35 years later

   D. 25 years later

4. Based on the timeline, which of the following statements is correct?

   A. Color television was demonstrated before the first full-length talking picture.

   B. Cell phones were invented before personal computers were introduced.

   C. The first transcontinental phone call was made during the 1800s.

   D. The first full-length talking picture came 20 years after the first transcontinental phone call.

5. On the timeline, an entry for Neil Armstrong walking on the moon would

  A. appear four years before Martin Cooper invented the first cell phone

  B. not appear because it happened during a different time frame

  C. not appear because it isn't a technological invention

  D. appear to the right of the entry for the first color television

6. Where would you place the invention of the World Wide Web on the timeline?

  A. before the invention of the cell phone

  B. after the introduction of the personal computer

  C. between the invention of the cell phone and the introduction of the personal computer

  D. at the beginning of the timeline

Write It Out Use what you have learned about a timeline to respond to the prompt below.

7. In the space below, create a timeline of your life. Include the most important events in your life, such as: the year you were born, the year you started school, the year you moved to a new school, the years your siblings were born, the year you started an activity or sport, and the year you visited a new city or state.

LESSON 5 — Making Inferences

WORDS TO KNOW   **Inference**   an educated guess based on what you are reading. When you make an inference, you are figuring out something the writer has not stated directly.

Review It!

Read these sentences. Use the Hint to help you understand the inference in the sentences.

In the photograph, Julius's smile is so wide you can see his usually hidden dimples. There is a twinkle in his eye.

Hint   Based on Julius's broad smile and the twinkle in his eye, you can infer that he was really happy when the photograph was taken.

Try It!

Read this passage. Underline the words that suggest a meaning not directly stated in the passage.

1   Juana was frustrated by the interruptions. She had been trying to finish her painting all week, but something kept getting in the way. Often it was her little brother, Carlos. When she heard him knocking on her door this time, she had to stop herself from shouting, "WHAT IS IT?"

2   "Yes?" Juana sighed, getting up from her desk. She wiped her hands on a paint-spotted towel as she opened the door. She looked out and saw her brother walking away. Something caught her attention on the floor. She looked down and saw that a bowl of her favorite cereal, a glass of orange juice, and a cup of hot mint tea were arranged nicely on a tray.

3   Juana smiled as she picked up the tray. She hadn't even noticed how hungry she was! She settled down at her desk and made room for her surprise meal.

Now, use the passage to answer the questions on the following page.

1. Based on the passage, you can infer that

   A. Juana and her brother fight a lot

   B. Juana is a really good painter

   C. Juana skipped breakfast that day

   D. Juana does not like painting very much

1.
Which answer choice seems possible but was not mentioned in the passage?

2. Juana's little brother is probably

   A. a little annoying   C. a painter like his sister

   B. a very good cook   D. looking for attention

3. Juana most likely had to wipe her hands on a towel before she could open the door because she

   A. had just washed her hands

   B. didn't want to spread germs

   C. had paint on her hands

   D. spilled some orange juice on her hands

3.
How would Juana's activity likely affect her hands?

4. During what time of day do you think this passage takes place?

   A. late afternoon   C. the middle of the night

   B. evening   D. late morning

In Your Own Words

5. Do you think Carlos made the meal for Juana? Who most likely helped him? What information in the passage supports your inference?

   _____

   _____

   _____

   _____

5.
Do you think Carlos would have been able to prepare the meal on the tray himself?

On Your Own!

Read this passage. Answer the questions that follow it.

Ellen could hear them downstairs. She knew they were there. Her mom had explained that they would be visiting soon, and she knew exactly how it would be. Pinched cheeks, big hugs, complicated questions that she didn't want to answer. "How is school?" "What do you want to be when you grow up?" All of those annoying, grown-up questions that she didn't need to hear yet. Ellen pulled the covers over her head, hoping she could hide all day. But then her father knocked at her door.

"I'm coming," she sighed.

Her father looked in and smiled. "They're not *that* bad," he said.

"Yes, they are, Dad. It's the same every time they visit. All these questions, as if I know what I want to be when I grow up. Can't I just be a kid? Can't I just stay here while you and Mom talk to them? I can dust off my old toys! I'll be quiet, I promise!"

"Sorry, El, but you need to be polite to our guests. Come on down for a little while. If it's unbearable, give me the signal, and I'll nod if it's okay for you to leave."

"Okay, Dad. I'll do my best. But really, why do you invite them over? It's torture!"

1. Based on the passage, you can infer that Ellen is hiding

   A. in her bed

   B. in the playroom

   C. at her desk

   D. with her mother

2. You can infer that Ellen is

   A. a very young child

   B. growing up faster than she would like

   C. secretly happy about the surprise guests

   D. hoping to avoid big hugs

3. The "signal" is probably something Ellen and her Dad

   A. made up so they could talk to each other on the phone

   B. only use when they are alone together

   C. heard about from friends and hope to use today for the first time

   D. use when they need to communicate privately in a larger group

4. You can infer that these days, Ellen plays with her old toys

   A. while watching TV

   B. very infrequently

   C. every day

   D. with guests

5. It's likely that the guests are

   A. Ellen's teenage cousins

   B. Ellen's school teachers

   C. Ellen's relatives

   D. children about Ellen's age

6. You can infer that Ellen would prefer to spend the day

   A. with her parents

   B. in the playroom

   C. alone in her room

   D. watching TV

Write It Out   Use the passage write a brief answer to the question below.

7. At the end of the passage, Ellen says, "Okay, Dad. I'll do my best. But really, why do you invite them over? It's torture!" What will she probably do next?

_____

_____

_____

_____

_____

LESSON
6 Drawing Conclusions

WORDS TO KNOW **Conclusion** an overall opinion that you form after reading a passage. A conclusion is based on what you've read but is not stated directly in the passage.

Review It! Read these sentences. Use the Hint to help you draw a conclusion.

My great-grandfather lives really far away, so I never see him. But I hear about him all the time. In fact, I was named after him. My parents are very excited because he's coming to visit soon.

Hint The parents talk about the boy's great-grandfather a lot. They also named their son after him. What conclusion can you draw about how the parents feel about the boy's great-grandfather?

Try It! Read this passage. <u>Underline</u> the sentences that suggest a meaning not directly stated in the passage.

(1) The boys had played well together their whole lives. Henry was three when his little brother, Theo, was born. They seemed to love each other right away. By the time Theo was walking, he was chasing his big brother everywhere. Henry would pick something up to play with, and Theo would decide he wanted to play with it. Henry would almost always hand it over.

(2) Later, when the boys were older, if Henry said he had a bad dream, Theo would start crying, saying his dreams were scary, too. Most of their friends couldn't understand it. They all disliked their sisters and brothers, or at least didn't want to hang around with them all the time.

(3) When the boys started to attend different schools, everyone worried. Henry was in grade school now, starting kindergarten. Theo was still in preschool. They only saw each other after school and on weekends. Their parents wondered if it would change their relationship.

Now, use the passage to answer the questions on the following page.

1. One conclusion you can draw from the passage is that

    A. Henry likes being a big brother

    B. the boys play well together

    C. Henry and Theo fight a lot

    D. Theo is in preschool

1.

Which answer choice states an overall opinion based on, but not directly stated in, the passage?

2. What conclusion can you draw based on paragraph 1?

    A. Theo had learned to walk.

    B. The boys sometimes have bad dreams.

    C. Henry is good at sharing.

    D. Henry was three when his brother was born.

3. One conclusion you can draw from paragraph 2 is that

    A. the boys didn't like to have friends over to play

    B. their friends didn't like their own sisters and brothers

    C. the boys only played with each other

    D. the boys spent time together even when friends were over

3.

How might the boys' friends learn about the boys' special bond?

4. From the last paragraph, you can conclude that

    A. everyone was worried about the boys going to different schools

    B. Henry was starting kindergarten in grade school

    C. their parents would give the boys extra time together on the weekends

    D. Theo would be in preschool for another year or so

In Your Own Words

5. What conclusion can you draw about the relationship between these brothers?

    _____

    _____

    _____

    _____

5.

What is your overall impression of the boys and how they feel about each other?

On Your Own!

Read this passage. Answer the questions that follow it.

Yvonne loved to swim. She loved the ocean most, but she also liked swimming in lakes. She and her mom went camping every year near a lake in the mountains, and she loved it because she could swim all day.

But Yvonne hated swimming pools. She didn't like the way the water felt. The chlorine was harsh and dried her hair and skin. She couldn't open her eyes under the water because it stung. Even if she could open her eyes, there was nothing interesting to look at on the bottom of a pool.

One day, Yvonne was asked to join the swim team. She was a strong swimmer and loved competition. She really wanted to prove that she could swim faster than anyone. But joining the swim team meant swimming in a *pool*.

Yvonne asked her mom, "What should I do?" She placed her chin in her hands and waited to hear what her mom would say.

"Make a list of pros and cons," her mom suggested. "That will help you sort out your reasons for and against joining the team."

Yvonne took her mom's advice. Her finished list had several pros, but only one con. "I guess it's pretty clear," said Yvonne. "There is just no way I can join the swim team!" And she ran into her room, crying.

---

1. Based on Yvonne's reaction in the last paragraph, you might conclude that

   A. Yvonne loves to swim
   B. Yvonne hates swimming in chlorine
   C. Yvonne won't join the swim team
   D. Yvonne loves to go camping

2. From the first two paragraphs, you can conclude that

   A. Yvonne likes to look at things on the bottom of lakes and oceans
   B. Yvonne hates swimming pools
   C. Yvonne doesn't want to be on the swim team
   D. Yvonne and her mother are very close

3. In the fourth paragraph, why does Yvonne place her chin in her hands?

   A. for a decision

   B. for advice

   C. for a ride to the pool

   D. for the fun of it

4. Which of the following can you conclude Yvonne wrote on the "cons" side of her paper?

   A. that she is a strong swimmer

   B. that she loves competition

   C. that she hates pools with chlorine

   D. that she doesn't like swimming indoors

5. At the end of the story, Yvonne's mother **most likely** feels

   A. confused

   B. excited

   C. worried

   D. happy

6. When Yvonne finishes her list and says, "I guess it's pretty clear," what does she **most likely** mean?

   A. She will decide to join the swim team when she realizes that pool water is clearer than lake water.

   B. She will decide to join the team because her list of "pros" is longer than her list of "cons."

   C. She will not join the swim team because pool water burns her eyes.

   D. She will join the swim team because she's a fast swimmer.

Write It Out Use the story to help you write a brief answer to the question below.

7. Yvonne makes a decision based on her list of pros and cons. There are several pros and only one con to joining the swim team. What can you conclude about how Yvonne feels about the items on the list?

   _____

   _____

   _____

   _____

LESSON 7 — Fact and Opinion

WORDS TO KNOW
Fact a statement that can be proven to be true
Opinion a statement of personal feeling or belief

Review It!

Read these sentences. Use the Hint to help you find a fact and an opinion.

The weather is warmest in the summer. That's why summer is the best time of year.

> **Hint** Which sentence can be proven to be true? Which sentence is a statement of personal feeling?

Try It!

Read this passage. <u>Underline</u> the sentences that state facts. Circle the sentences that state opinions.

(1) Zina Garrison was the best tennis player ever. She may not have won every big title, but that was just bad luck.

(2) Garrison was born in Houston, Texas, in 1963. She experienced a lot of personal tragedy in her childhood. Her father and older brother both died when she was a baby. Then, when Zina was a teenager, her mother died. But she kept working hard anyway. Garrison helped the United States win a gold medal in the 1988 Olympics!

(3) Since she stopped playing tennis, Garrison has worked to make the world a better place. She founded the Zina Garrison All-Court Tennis Program in 1992. This program brings tennis to inner-city kids in Houston. She also founded the Zina Garrison Foundation for the Homeless in 1988. So, she may not have won every match she played. But she has had a huge impact on her community and on the world. That's why she is the best tennis player ever!

Now, use the passage to answer the questions on the following page.

1. Which sentence from the passage expresses a fact?

   A. "Zina Garrison was the best tennis player ever."

   B. "She may not have won every big title, but that was just bad luck."

   C. "Garrison was born in Houston, Texas, in 1963."

   D. "That's why she is the best tennis player ever!"

2. Which sentence from the passage expresses an opinion?

   A. "She experienced a lot of personal tragedy in her childhood."

   B. "Her father and older brother both died when she was a baby."

   C. "She founded the Zina Garrison Foundation for the Homeless in 1988."

   D. "But she has had a huge impact on her community and on the world."

3. Which is an opinion with which the author of this passage would **most likely** agree?

   A. Zina Garrison was the youngest in a family of seven children.

   B. Zina Garrison should be honored as the best tennis player in history.

   C. Zina Garrison played very good tennis but didn't win many matches.

   D. Zina Garrison has served on several committees about sports.

4. Which of the following is the **best** source for finding more facts about Zina Garrison and other tennis players of her time?

   A. the Zina Garrison Fan Club website

   B. Zina Garrison's biography

   C. the sports history section of the library

   D. an article about the 1988 Olympic Games

In Your Own Words

5. List three facts from the passage.

   _____

   _____

   _____

Ask Yourself

1.
Which of the answer choices could you prove by looking in an encyclopedia or checking reputable sources on the Internet?

3.
Which answer choice states a personal belief that cannot be proven, and with which some people might disagree?

5.
Did you underline the facts in the passage as you read? Are you sure they can be proven?

On Your Own!

Read this passage. Answer the questions that follow it.

Cross-country skiing has been around for a long time. But it wasn't always a sport. Skis were once used only to help people get around in the snow. The oldest known skis were short and wide. They looked nothing like the skis we use today. These ancient skis were found in Sweden and are over 4,500 years old. Maybe cross-country skiing should have stayed in the past. It is not an enjoyable sport!

Back in the 1700s, there was no difference between cross-country and downhill skiing. All skis had boots with a toe-mount, so that the skier's heels were free to move up and down. Today, this is only true in cross-country skiing. And it's a problem, because the toe-mount makes your foot feel like it could slide right out of the ski. It only adds to the skier's fears of falling down.

By the early 1800s, the sport of skiing had grown to include ski races and ski jump competitions. But there was still no difference between cross-country and down-hill skiing. Unfortunately, skiing became more popular in the early 1900s. The first Olympic winter games, in France in 1924, had only five sports. Skiing played a major role. Too bad, because then even more people learned about skiing.

Cross-country skiing became a stand-alone Olympic event in the 1932 Winter Games in Lake Placid, New York. This is when the distinction between the two types of skiing became clearest. It's unfortunate, because cross-country skiing is such a waste of time.

1. **Which sentence from the first paragraph contains an opinion?**

   A. "Cross-country skiing has been around for a long time."

   B. "It is not an enjoyable sport!"

   C. "The oldest known skis were short and wide."

   D. "These ancient skis were found in Sweden and are over 4,500 years old."

2. **Which sentence states a fact from the passage?**

   A. "But there was still no difference between cross-country and downhill skiing."

   B. "It's unfortunate, because cross-country skiing is such a waste of time."

   C. "Maybe cross-country skiing should have stayed in the past."

   D. "It is not an enjoyable sport!"

3. Which states an opinion with which the author of this passage would **most likely** agree?

   A. Cross-country skiing is one of the best winter activities.

   B. Cross-country skiing has a long and interesting history.

   C. Cross-country skiing is a lot like downhill skiing, except for the boots.

   D. Cross-country skiing is scary because sometimes you can fall down.

4. Which sentence from the passage is an opinion?

   A. "Cross-country skiing has been around for a long time."

   B. "Skiing played a major role."

   C. "It's unfortunate, because cross-country skiing is such a waste of time."

   D. "Today, this is only true in cross-country skiing."

5. Which of the following is a fact from the passage?

   A. The first known skis were found in Sweden.

   B. Ancient skis were wide and unsafe.

   C. Toe-mounted ski boots added to the skier's fears of falling down.

   D. Downhill ski boots should have toe-mounts.

6. Which is a fact from the last paragraph of the passage?

   A. Skiing played a major role in the 1924 Olympics.

   B. Cross-country skiing is a waste of everyone's time.

   C. The difference between the two types of skiing became clear in 1932.

   D. Skiing became a stand-alone event in the 1924 Olympics in Lake Placid.

Write It Out   Use the passage to help you write a brief answer to the question below.

7. The passage states, "Unfortunately, skiing became more popular in the early 1900s." Does this sentence express a fact, an opinion, or both? Explain your answer.

_____

_____

_____

_____

LESSON 8 · Essential and Nonessential Information

WORDS TO KNOW

Essential information   information that is connected directly to the topic of the passage

Nonessential information   information that is not important to the topic of the passage

---

Review It!

Read these sentences. Use the Hint to help you find the essential information.

The park is a great place to ride bikes, fly kites, or walk dogs. It was really hot yesterday. The park is open from sunrise to sunset, all summer long.

> **Hint**   Which sentences give information about the park that visitors would most need to know?

Try It!

Read this passage. <u>Underline</u> the sentences that state essential information about the topic. Circle the nonessential information.

(1)   Collages are fun to make. You just need a few things and a lot of imagination. First, you'll need to get the following things together:

- Piece of cardboard
- Colorful paper
- Dry pasta
- Magazines
- Scissors
- Glue stick
- Bottle of glue

(2)   I once made a happy collage. It had a lot of red and pink in it. I felt happy that day.

(3)   Protect your table by covering it with newspaper. Look through the magazines and cut out the pictures that you like. Then start gluing things to the cardboard. See where your imagination takes you!

(4)   You can make a great collage. All you need is some time, some imagination, and some simple materials. You can add other things too, like buttons, greeting cards, and glitter. I know you can make one as nice as mine!

Now, use the passage to answer the questions on the following page.

1. Which sentence from the passage is nonessential?

   A. "First, you'll need to get the following things together."

   B. "Collages are fun to make."

   C. "I once made a happy collage."

   D. "You just need a few things and a lot of imagination."

2. Which sentence from the passage is essential?

   A. "It had a lot of red and pink in it."

   B. "I felt happy that day."

   C. "I know you can make one as nice as mine!"

   D. "Then start gluing things to the cardboard."

1.
Which answer choice could be deleted without changing the main idea of the passage?

3. Which of the following information would be **most** important if you wanted to know how to make a collage?

   A. what materials to use

   B. how other people feel when they make collages

   C. the history of collages

   D. why someone else decided to make a collage one time

3.
Which answer choice relates to the main idea of the passage?

4. Which of the following information would be considered nonessential to someone who wanted to make a collage?

   A. the best type of glue to use for gluing pasta to paper

   B. how the writer felt the day she wrote the directions for making a collage

   C. the best materials to use for making a collage

   D. how to get set up to make a collage

In Your Own Words

5. What information in the passage is nonessential? Tell why it is nonessential. What would you add to make the passage better?

_____

_____

_____

_____

5.
Look back at the nonessential information you circled in the passage. How is it different from essential information?

On Your Own!

Read this passage. Answer the questions that follow it.

African elephants live in the grasslands of Africa. They are large animals with long tusks and great big flapping ears. Elephants are famous for their long trunks, with which they eat, bathe, and dig wells! Elephants are also known for their keen sense of hearing. But elephants can't see very well at all. Their eyes are very small. Anteaters also have small eyes. Elephants also have a very good memory. A female elephant can lead her herd to a watering hole she hasn't visited in 30 years! All animals in Africa must be able to find watering holes to survive.

Asian elephants are different from African elephants. Male Asian elephants grow tusks, but females do not. Male walruses also have tusks. Asian elephants are smaller than African elephants. Their ears are smaller and shaped differently. Some people say that the African elephant's ear is shaped like the continent of Africa. I wonder if the Asian elephant's ear is shaped like India. Asian elephants also grow more hair on their bodies. All mammals grow hair.

It might surprise you to learn that African and Asian elephants are related to an animal that lives in the ocean. Manatees are ocean-dwelling mammals, like whales. But unlike whales, manatees have toenails. Those toenails are just like an elephant's toenails! And their noses are like short trunks. Some dinosaurs had short trunks, as well. And manatee skin is similar to elephant skin. Maybe manatees and elephants have an ancestor in common. My ancestors are from Scotland.

1. Which sentence from the first paragraph contains nonessential information?

   A. "African elephants live in the grasslands of Africa."

   B. "Elephants are also known for their keen sense of hearing."

   C. "Anteaters also have small eyes."

   D. "Elephants also have a very good memory."

2. Which sentence from the second paragraph contains essential information?

   A. "Male walruses also have tusks."

   B. "I wonder if the Asian elephant's ear is shaped like India."

   C. "All mammals grow hair."

   D. "Asian elephants are smaller than African elephants."

3. Which sentence from the third paragraph contains nonessential information?

   A. "Some dinosaurs had short trunks, as well."

   B. "Manatees are ocean-dwelling mammals, like whales."

   C. "But unlike whales, manatees have toenails."

   D. "And manatee skin is similar to elephant skin."

4. Which information from the passage would be important for a paper about Asian elephants?

   A. "African elephants live in the grasslands of Africa."

   B. "Male Asian elephants grow tusks, but females do not."

   C. "Manatees are ocean-dwelling mammals, like whales."

   D. "I wonder if the Asian elephant's ear is shaped like India."

5. Read the following sentence from the passage.

   > It might surprise you to learn that African and Asian elephants are related to an animal that lives in the ocean.

   Why did the author **most likely** include this information in the passage?

   A. to show the difference between African and Asian elephants

   B. to explain that African and Asian elephants probably have a similar ancestor

   C. to show the difference between elephants and whales

   D. to begin a comparison between elephants and manatees

6. Which of the following is nonessential information from the passage?

   A. "My ancestors are from Scotland."

   B. "Maybe manatees and elephants have an ancestor in common."

   C. "Manatees are ocean-dwelling mammals, like whales."

   D. "Elephants are also known for their keen sense of hearing."

Write It Out   Use the passage to help you write a brief answer to the question below.

7. The passage states, "I wonder if the Asian elephant's ear is shaped like India." Is this an example of essential or nonessential information? Explain your answer.

   _____

   _____

   _____

LESSON 9 · Elements of a Good Argument

WORDS TO KNOW | **Argument** the writer's position on a topic, including how the writer feels about the topic and reasons why

---

Review It!

Read this sentence. Use the Hint to help you figure out the writer's argument.

People need to change their ways in order for our natural resources to last us into the next generation.

> **Hint** The writer believes that the overuse of natural resources is a problem. But this sentence alone is not an argument. What evidence could be added to support this position?

Try It!

Now, read the complete passage below. <u>Underline</u> the sentences that support the writer's argument.

1. To the Editor:

2. People need to change their ways, or our natural resources won't last. We must reduce the amount of energy we use. We must drive less, fly less, and heat and cool our homes more responsibly. Our most common energy sources, like natural gas, are not renewable resources. When they run out, they will be gone forever.

3. There may come a day when only the rich will be able to drive and cool their houses in summer. Don't let that happen! Here's what you can do:
   - Drive less, ride bicycles, or use public transportation!
   - Fly less. Do Americans need to travel? Stay home! Learn about local culture.
   - Lower thermostats by 3 degrees in winter; raise them by 3 degrees in summer.

4. Try to use less energy each day. This will help our resources last longer.

Sincerely,

Rosa Martinez

Now, use the passage to answer the questions on the following page.

1. What is the writer's position in this letter to the editor?

   A. We use too much energy and have to make changes.

   B. Gasoline is an important resource for this country.

   C. People should drive and fly less often.

   D. We heat and cool our houses too much.

1.

Which answer choice states the main idea of the letter, and not a detail from it?

2. Which of the following is an example of evidence the writer uses to back up her argument?

   A. "Drive less, ride bicycles, or use public transportation!"

   B. "We must reduce the amount of energy we use."

   C. "Our most common energy sources, like natural gas, are not renewable resources."

   D. "Do Americans need to travel?"

3. The writer is trying to persuade readers to

   A. reduce, reuse, and recycle

   B. change the way they use energy

   C. drive smaller cars

   D. stop taking long trips

3.

Which answer choice best summarizes the writer's main point in her letter?

4. Which sentence from the letter states the writer's point of view most clearly?

   A. "When they run out, they will be gone forever."

   B. "Drive less, ride bicycles, or use public transportation!"

   C. "We must reduce the amount of energy we use."

   D. "There may come a day when only the rich will be able to drive and cool their houses in summer."

In Your Own Words

5. Does the writer present a convincing argument for her viewpoint? Explain your answer.

   _____

   _____

   _____

5.

Does the writer back up her opinion with facts? Does she present evidence that convinces you to make changes?

On Your Own!

Read this passage. Answer the questions that follow it.

To the Editor:

Many of you are too young to remember when the law required people to pick up after their dogs. Unfortunately, not everyone followed the law. Growing up, I remember sidestepping "packages" all over the sidewalk on my way to school. Maybe if today's young dog walkers had lived through this, they would be more thoughtful.

We've all seen someone walking a dog without a plastic bag in his or her hands. We have all seen a dog owner looking in the other direction while his dog deposits a "package" on the sidewalk. No one likes to see that mess!

I propose that we ask the mayor to put up plastic-bag dispensers on popular dog-walking paths. We should place one every few hundred feet, with a sign reminding dog-walkers to clean up after their pets. It can make all the difference.

You're probably thinking that the dispensers would empty out right away. I propose asking the mayor to assign this responsibility to the director of the city's dog pound. He could patrol the streets every week and refill the dispensers. Maybe local schools could have doggie-bag collection drives!

If we don't take this matter into our own hands and force the mayor to do something, we will be sidestepping "packages" again and again.

Yours truly,

James Conti

1. What is the writer's position in this letter to the editor?

   A. All dog walkers are young and irresponsible.

   B. The mayor should do a better job.

   C. Plastic-bag dispensers would help keep the streets clean.

   D. People should think about the elderly more often.

2. What is the writer's main argument?

   A. Dog walkers are creating a mess in the city because they don't pick after their dogs.

   B. Some people did not pick up after their dogs when they were kids.

   C. The director of the city pound should patrol the streets for "packages."

   D. Local schools could have doggie-bag collection drives.

3. Which sentence from the passage is evidence that supports the writer's argument?

   A. "Many of you are too young to remember when the law required people to pick up after their dogs."

   B. "I propose that we ask the mayor to put up plastic-bag dispensers on popular dog-walking paths."

   C. "Maybe if today's young dog walkers had lived through this, they would be more thoughtful."

   D. "We have all seen a dog owner looking in the other direction while his dog deposits a 'package' on the sidewalk."

4. The writer is trying to persuade readers to

   A. ask dog walkers to pick up after their pets

   B. get the director of the dog pound to refill the plastic-bag dispensers when making his rounds

   C. pick up after their dogs

   D. get the mayor to install plastic-bag dispensers along popular dog-walking routes

5. The writer's argument would be more effective if it contained more

   A. tales from his childhood

   B. evidence of the problem

   C. advice for dog walkers

   D. ideas about possible solutions

6. The strongest part of the writer's argument is that

   A. no one likes to see a mess on the sidewalk

   B. most readers are too young to remember what it used to be like

   C. the dispensers would empty out right away

   D. young people are not very thoughtful

Write It Out Use the passage to help you write a brief answer to the question below.

7. Does the writer present a convincing argument for his viewpoint? Explain your answer.

_____

_____

_____

LESSON 10 Using Research

WORDS TO KNOW

Research finding information for a certain purpose

Sources books, encyclopedias, articles, and websites that contain information about the topic you are researching

---

Review It! Read these sentences. Use the Hint to help you decide if the source is reliable.

Aliens were spotted landing in a giant cornfield last night near Wichita, Kansas. Local observers watched the flying saucers land a little after midnight, but did not report seeing any small green men.

> **Hint** Reliable information can be backed up by several different, trustworthy sources. Does this passage seem as if it comes from a reliable source?

Try It! Read this passage. Underline the topic for research.

(1) Leilani has to write a report. She has to write about her favorite U.S. president. But Leilani isn't from the United States. She doesn't know which president to write about. Her teacher said Leilani could choose any president in history. She doesn't need to limit her research to recent presidents.

(2) Leilani feels lost. She went to the library to do a search on the computer. She is looking for articles that will help her find a good subject. Here is her search:

- Search Item: U.S. Presidents
- Articles Found: 40,604

(3) There is no way she can read that many articles! She wouldn't have any time left over to write the report. She needs to limit her search, but how?

Now, use the passage to answer the questions on the following page.

1. What should Leilani do to narrow down her search?

   A. read as many articles about U.S. presidents as she can

   B. decide on one aspect of each president to compare

   C. make a list of all U.S. presidents and pick one randomly

   D. write a report on U.S. history instead

1.

Which answer choice would create a search that would turn up fewer results?

2. Which phrase might Leilani use in her next search?

   A. U.S. presidents with good foreign-relations ratings

   B. U.S. presidents from the United States

   C. U.S. presidents in history

   D. U.S. presidents who were inspiring

3. Which source could Leilani use to help her choose a president to write about?

   A. an encyclopedia entry about one president

   B. a local newspaper

   C. a book about how presidents are elected

   D. a magazine article comparing U.S. presidents

3.

Which source would best provide general information about several U.S. presidents?

4. Once she decides on a president to write about, Leilani should

   A. read one article and write the report from the information she learns

   B. read several reliable articles and books about the president she chooses

   C. check out a book about that president and read the whole thing

   D. scan the Internet for funny stories about that president

In Your Own Words

5. If you had to write this report, what keywords or phrases would you type into the search engine on your library's computer? What would you do with the results?

_____

_____

_____

5.

What do presidents do that seem most important to you?

On Your Own!

Read this passage. Answer the questions that follow it.

Jason has to write a report for his history class about the settlement in Jamestown, Virginia. His first search brought up more results than he had time to look through. He decided to narrow his subject down. Now he is researching how the settlement in Jamestown affected the local Native American tribe, the Powhatans.

But there are so many interesting things about the Powhatans. Jason is having a hard time staying focused on his subject. He wants to read all of the articles about Powhatan leaders, lifestyles, cooking habits, and hunting techniques. He forgot his assignment was to write about how the settlement affected the Powhatans.

Jason has a lot of sources in front of him as he sits down to write his report. He is looking at an article with drawings of a Powhatan village. He is reading about how five-year-old Powhatan boys were allowed to hunt with their own bows and arrows. Jason is now on-line, looking at the Jamestown website, historicjamestowne.org, hoping he and his family can plan a trip to visit the museum there.

1. Which source will help Jason get focused again?

   A. a website about the history of all of the European settlements in North America

   B. an article about the relationship between settlers and Native Americans in early Virginia

   C. an article called "Powhatan Princess: The Real Pocahontas"

   D. a textbook chapter about the lives of the settlers in the first 13 colonies

2. Which phrase could Jason use to focus his search on his chosen topic?

   A. Jamestown settlers and lifestyles

   B. Settlers and Native Americans in the United States

   C. Powhatan conflict with settlers in Jamestown

   D. Powhatan hunting techniques

3. Which would be the **most** trustworthy source for Jason's report?

   A. a current local newspaper from Jamestown, Virginia

   B. a friend's description of her visit to the Jamestown museum and the Powhatan village

   C. an article on the Internet about Powhatan culture

   D. an encyclopedia entry about settlers and Native Americans in Jamestown

4. To help Jason focus, which of these articles should he remove from his desk?

   A. "Settlers and Native Americans in Early Virginia"

   B. "Powhatan Hunting: Five-Year-Old Boys Hunt with the Tribe"

   C. "Powhatan Indians: How They Greeted the Settlers"

   D. "Virginia Settlers Fight Powhatans for Power"

5. The Jamestown website might have helpful information. Which of the following links should Jason click on?

   A. exhibits

   B. visiting

   C. history

   D. contact

6. Jason found a link called "resources" on the Jamestown website. Which of these sources might help him with his report?

   A. Jamestown Ceramic Research Group (a description of 17th-century ceramics)

   B. Jamestown 2007 Conference (a comparison of several 17th-century sites in the region)

   C. Interactive Exercises (activities to discover how archaeology is done at Jamestown)

   D. Journal of the Jamestown Rediscovery Center (research about early European settlement of North America)

Write It Out   Use the passage to help you write a brief answer to the question below.

7. Would the historicjamestowne.org website be a trustworthy source? Explain your answer.

_____

_____

_____

_____

LESSON 11 Understanding Format

WORDS TO KNOW **Format** how text is arranged and organized. Features such as the title, table of contents, headings, glossary, and index help the reader understand the organization of a text and the information it contains.

Read this index. Use the Hint to help you understand how to use an index.

banana bread, 11
bread (whole grain), 23–29
fruit tarts, 13
muffins, 21
waffles, 5

Hint An index is found at the back of a book. This index is from a cookbook. If you wanted to bake muffins, you would turn to page 21.

Try It! Read this table of contents. A table of contents is found at the beginning of a book. It lists the chapters in the book along with the page numbers on which each chapter begins.

Now, use the table of contents to answer the questions on the following page.

1. Chapter 3 begins on

A. page 3   **C.** page 14

B. page 7   **D.** page 23

2. In which chapter would you look to find information about how Kwanzaa is similar to celebrations in Africa?

A. Chapter 1   **C.** Chapter 3

B. Chapter 2   **D.** Chapter 4

3. In which chapter would you look to find information about when the first Kwanzaa celebration took place?

A. Chapter 1   **C.** Chapter 3

B. Chapter 2   **D.** Chapter 4

4. What is **most likely** discussed on pages 3 through 6?

A. the history of Kwanzaa

B. general information about Kwanzaa

C. Kwanzaa's importance in Africa

D. how Kwanzaa is celebrated around the world

In Your Own Words

5. This table of contents comes from a particular book. What is the book about? What might be a good title for it?

_____

_____

_____

_____

Ask Yourself

1.
If you pass your finger over the line about Chapter 3, what page number does it land on?

3.
Which chapter title mentions something about the history of Kwanzaa?

5.
What word is repeated in each of the chapter titles?

On Your Own!

Read this passage. Answer the questions that follow it.

Introduction

Knitting is one way of making yarn into cloth. A knitter loops yarn through stitches on a set of knitting needles. This makes a length of cloth, such as a scarf. Knitters can stitch pieces of cloth together to make a sweater or gloves. They can also knit on a circular needle to make hats and socks.

Knit and Purl Stitches

There are two common types of stitches in knitting. They look different because the yarn is pulled through the stitch in a different direction. The "knit" stitch looks like a "V." The "purl" stitch looks like a wavy line. Combining knit and purl stitches in different ways makes a pattern in the cloth.

Cables

Sometimes sweaters and scarves have more complicated patterns. A knitter can knit a few stitches onto a very short needle, and then cross them over other stitches. This forms a cable pattern. It looks like braided hair. Cables make the cloth thicker, and therefore warmer.

Additions

Knitters can add other things to a cloth. They can thread buttons and beads onto the yarn before making a stitch. They can also pull loops out to create a shaggy look. A creative knitter can decorate a cloth in many ways!

---

1. What would be the **best** title for this passage?

   A. "A Guide to Knitting"

   B. "The History of Knitting"

   C. "An Introduction to Knitting Cables"

   D. "Some Brief Details about Knitting"

2. Read the following sentence.

   > Many sweaters have a pattern of "knit one, purl one" along the wrists and waistline.

   Under which heading from the passage would this sentence **best** fit?

   A. Introduction

   B. Knit and Purl Stitches

   C. Cables

   D. Additions

3. Read the following sentence.

   Many heavy winter sweaters have cable patterns knitted into them.

   Under which heading from the passage would this sentence **best** fit?

   A. Introduction

   B. Knit and Purl Stitches

   C. Cables

   D. Additions

4. What would be a better heading for the last section of the passage?

   A. Decorations

   B. Patterns

   C. Knitting

   D. Colors

5. This passage is part of a longer book about different kinds of crafts. In which chapter would you expect to find this passage?

   A. Chapter 1: An Introduction to the Sewing Arts

   B. Chapter 3: Crocheting and Hooking

   C. Chapter 6: What Can't You Make with Thread?

   D. Chapter 9: How Yarn Becomes Cloth

6. If you wanted to learn more about this topic, which of the following index entries would you select?

   A. crochet hooks, 34

   B. sewing machines, 12

   C. knitting, 79

   D. threads and yarn, 10

Write It Out   Use the passage to help you write brief answers to the questions below.

7. How do the headings help you understand the information presented in the passage? How would that be different without the headings?

   _____

   _____

   _____

   _____

   _____

   _____

LESSON 12 ▷ Cause and Effect

WORDS TO KNOW

Cause the reason why something happens

Effect something that happens as the result of a cause

Review It!

Read these sentences. Use the Hint to help you understand the cause and effect.

George was hungry. He went to the fridge and found a carton of yogurt, which he ate quickly.

> **Hint** Why did George eat a carton of yogurt? Because he was hungry. What is the cause? What is the effect?

Try It!

Read this passage. As you read, think about causes and effects in the story.

(1) Gilda did not like summer. She did not like to be hot. She was happiest in the winter. But since it couldn't be winter all the time, she found ways to make herself feel comfortable in the summer. She stayed inside, in the air conditioning, as much as she could. She always wore loose-fitting clothing. She never exercised outdoors.

(2) One summer day Gilda's mother asked her to spend the afternoon with her little brother, Max. Max liked to play outside. The heat didn't bother him at all.

(3) "Don't you want to ride bikes?" Max asked. "No way," Gilda answered.

(4) "Let's walk to the restaurant for lunch," Gilda suggested. "No way!" said Max.

(5) The siblings stood face-to-face, angry at each other. Then Gilda had an idea. "I know!" Gilda said, excited now. "Let's go swimming!" Max happily agreed, and they both ran upstairs to put on their swimsuits.

Now, use the passage to answer the questions on the following page.

1. Why does Gilda wear loose-fitting clothing in the summer?

   A. It helps her stay cool.

   B. It is more comfortable than tight clothes.

   C. Her mother tells her to.

   D. She can exercise easily in loose clothing.

1.

What causes Gilda to choose this type of clothing?

2. Gilda dislikes summer because

   A. she hates to exercise

   B. she doesn't like swimming

   C. she hates to sweat

   D. she doesn't like riding bikes

3. What causes the disagreement between Gilda and her brother?

   A. Gilda wants to ride bikes.

   B. Max wants to eat in a restaurant.

   C. They can't agree where to go swimming.

   D. They can't agree about how to spend the afternoon.

4. What is the effect of Gilda's last suggestion?

   A. Max wants to come up with a different idea.

   B. Gilda is happy now.

   C. Max won't go out to eat.

   D. Gilda and Max are both excited.

4.

What is Gilda's last suggestion? How does this make the characters behave?

In Your Own Words

5. Gilda doesn't like the heat. How does that fact affect everything else that happens in the story?

   _____

   _____

   _____

   _____

5.

What does Gilda do to stay cool?

On Your Own!

Read this passage. Answer the questions that follow it.

Arriving at camp, Juan felt sad. He had never been away from his parents overnight. He wasn't sure he liked the idea of staying at sleep-away camp for a week. Some of his friends were there too, but Juan still felt lonely. The first night, he barely slept. When he got up for breakfast, he didn't feel hungry. He walked over to the cafeteria alone, watching his friends run ahead of him.

When Juan arrived at the cafeteria, the place was a mess. Food was everywhere. The cooks were yelling. The campers were laughing. There had been a food fight! Juan was shocked. His parents had told him to be on his best behavior at camp. He couldn't believe the other campers would act this way.

Juan walked into the kitchen. "EXCUSE ME!" he yelled over the noise. When the cooks turned around, they were surprised to see Juan. "Would you like some help cleaning up?" Juan asked.

"That would be great!" the cooks said. Together they started cleaning up the mess in the kitchen. Then they went out to the cafeteria tables and asked everyone to quiet down. Watching Juan, the other campers started to feel bad. They were sorry they'd caused such a mess. They started to help, too. Pretty soon, the cafeteria looked good, and breakfast was served—again. Juan was proud that he'd helped. Maybe camp would be an okay place, after all.

---

1. At the beginning of the story Juan feels sad because he

   A. doesn't like the food they serve at camp

   B. doesn't have any friends at camp

   C. feels lonely at sleep-away camp

   D. hates food fights

2. What is the cause of the mess in the cafeteria?

   A. There was a food fight.

   B. The cooks had an argument.

   C. Juan dropped his food.

   D. The campers are messy eaters.

3. What causes Juan to walk into the kitchen and offer to help the cooks?

   A. His friends tell him to.

   B. He remembers what his parents said.

   C. His camp leader makes him go.

   D. The cooks call to him.

4. Why does Juan have to yell to get the cooks' attention?

   A. He is very short and no one sees him.

   B. Someone is vacuuming up the mess.

   C. The cooks are fighting with one another.

   D. The other campers are making a lot of noise.

5. What is the effect of Juan's offer to help clean up?

   A. The cooks punish the campers.

   B. The campers have a food fight.

   C. Everyone is able to eat the food Juan cooked.

   D. The other campers feel bad and start to help.

6. What effect does cleaning up the food fight **most likely** have on Juan?

   A. He decides to leave camp early.

   B. He thinks camp might turn out okay in the end.

   C. He feels ashamed that he made such a mess.

   D. He calls home to tell his parents he is lonely.

Write It Out Use the story to help you write a brief answer to the question below.

7. The food fight is an important event in the story. What are some of the effects of that event?

_____

_____

_____

_____

LESSON 13 Compare and Contrast

WORDS TO KNOW **Compare** to show how things are alike, or similar
Contrast to show how things are different

Review It!

Read these sentences. Use the Hint to help you compare and contrast the information.

The twins both had red hair, green eyes, and freckles. But while Jenny was bossy, Jamie was sweet and generous.

> **Hint** The author uses the word *both* when she tells how the twins are alike. She uses the words *but* and *while* to tell how they are different.

Try It!

Read this passage. As you read, look for ways the people are alike and ways they are different.

1. There are four siblings in my family. I am the oldest. My name is Anne. My sister Elizabeth was born next. My brother Morgan is after her and then, the youngest, Suzy.

2. Morgan and I like to play ice hockey. Dad teaches us on the weekends. Elizabeth and Suzy think ice hockey is silly. They would rather go hiking. Suzy is the one who likes to ride horses. She wishes we could own a horse! Mom tells her to keep dreaming. I'm allergic to horses, which is fine, because I hate them! I can't even eat dinner with Suzy after she comes home from a lesson. I sneeze the whole time!

3. Now there's one thing we all agree on: dinner! Mom is the best cook in the world, and we all look forward to sitting down at the dinner table together every night.

Now, use the passage to answer the questions on the following page.

1. How are Anne and Suzy alike?

   A. They both love horses.

   B. They both like to go hiking.

   C. They both love ice hockey.

   D. They are both girls.

1.

Which answer choice states something Anne and Suzy have in common, even if it isn't stated directly in the passage?

2. How are Anne and Morgan alike?

   A. They both play ice hockey.

   B. They both hate horses.

   C. They are the same age.

   D. They are twins.

3. One way Suzy and Elizabeth are different is that

   A. they think ice hockey is silly

   B. only one of them is the youngest

   C. they like to go for hikes

   D. only one of them is allergic to horses

3.

The question asks about differences, not similarities. Which answer choices state differences between the two sisters? Which answer is best supported by the passage?

4. One thing all the siblings have in common is that

   A. they all play ice hockey

   B. they all love dinner

   C. they all take riding lessons

   D. they all like to go hiking

In Your Own Words

5. Name two similarities and two differences between some of the siblings mentioned in the passage.

   _____

   _____

   _____

   _____

5.

What do the siblings have in common? In what ways are they different from each other?

On Your Own!

Read this passage. Answer the questions that follow it.

The phrase "martial arts" describes a type of hand-to-hand sport that began long ago in the Far East. In the beginning, these sports were used to train soldiers to fight in war. Today, people train in martial arts for physical exercise and mental well-being.

Aikido comes from Japan and isn't as old as other martial arts. It combines movement, spirituality, and nonviolence. This martial art teaches hand-to-hand fighting methods, but it was never used to train soldiers. It teaches the student how to combine martial arts with a journey to better understand the world. It is thought to be a gentle martial art that focuses on self-defense.

Karate originally comes from China and is known for striking, punching, and kicking. This martial art was used to train soldiers. Many consider Karate to be a more violent martial art. Like Aikido, it seeks to train people to be gentle. It also prepares people to defend themselves, if they need to.

Tai Chi also comes from China. This martial art is very different from Aikido and Karate. Tai Chi looks like it is happening in slow motion. Groups of people practice it together, though they never come into contact with one another. Tai Chi is the only slow and relaxed martial art. Its goal of understanding the larger world, however, is shared by most other martial arts.

---

1. **How are Aikido and Karate alike?**

   A. They were both used to train soldiers.

   B. They both come from Japan.

   C. They both teach methods of self-defense.

   D. They both look like they happen in slow motion.

2. **How are Karate and Tai Chi alike?**

   A. They both come from China.

   B. The both involve kicking and punching.

   C. They are both slow and relaxed.

   D. They both involve hand-to-hand fighting.

3. Which of the following is something the passage states all three martial arts have in common?

   A. They are all from China.

   B. They are all practiced in large groups.

   C. They were all developed to train soldiers.

   D. They share a goal of understanding the larger world.

4. Which of the following describes a difference between Karate and Aikido?

   A. Aikido was never used to train soldiers, while Karate was.

   B. Karate offers self-defense, while Aikido does not.

   C. Aikido comes from ancient China, and Karate from old Japan.

   D. Karate is well known for its gentle nature, but Aikido is not.

5. Which of the following lists the three martial arts in order from least violent to more violent?

   A. Aikido, Karate, Tai Chi

   B. Karate, Aikido, Tai Chi

   C. Tai Chi, Karate, Aikido

   D. Tai Chi, Aikido, Karate

6. One important difference that sets Tai Chi apart from the other two martial arts described in the passage is that Tai Chi

   A. is done slowly, in groups

   B. isn't as old as the others

   C. comes from Japan

   D. teaches self-defense

Write It Out Use the passage to help you write a response to the prompt below.

7. Based on the information in the passage, draw a graphic organizer that represents the similarities and differences between these three martial arts.

LESSON 14 Sequence

WORDS TO KNOW **Sequence** the order in which events happen in an informational passage or a story. Sequence is also called "chronological order."

Review It!

Read these sentences. Use the Hint to help you follow the sequence of events.

First, mix the flour, baking soda, and salt together. Next, beat the eggs and add them to the milk. Finally, mix the wet and dry ingredients together.

> **Hint** Words such as *first*, *next*, and *finally* help you keep track of the order of events in a passage.

Try It!

Read this passage. As you read, think about the order in which the information is presented.

To make your own kaleidoscope, you will need to gather these materials: 3 narrow mirrors (each about 1 1/2 inches wide), 1 paper-towel tube, 1 empty ribbon spool, 1 small plastic dish, glue, tape, and markers.

Next, follow these steps:

- Place the mirrors together to form a triangle.
- Tape the edges together.
- Slide the triangle into the paper-towel tube.
- Tape the ribbon spool to one end of the paper-towel tube. This will be the eyepiece.
- Draw lines and shapes on the inside of the plastic dish with the markers. Use as many different colors as you can.
- Glue the plastic dish to the open end of the tube.

Now, use the passage to answer the questions on the following page.

1. According to the passage, what should you do **first** in order to make a kaleidoscope?

   A. Gather the materials.

   B. Put the mirrors together.

   C. Glue the plastic dish to the tube.

   D. Draw on the inside of the plastic dish.

2. What step comes **after** placing the mirrors together?

   A. sliding the triangle into the tube

   B. taping the ribbon spool to one end

   C. taping the edges of the mirrors together

   D. drawing on the inside of the plastic dish

3. What step comes **before** gluing the plastic dish to the end of the tube?

   A. taping the ribbon spool to the other end

   B. gathering the materials together

   C. looking through your new kaleidoscope

   D. drawing on the inside of the plastic dish

4. Which of the following would be the **best** final step, after gluing the plastic dish to the end of the tube?

   A. cleaning up all the materials

   B. looking through your new kaleidoscope

   C. gluing the ribbon spool to the other end

   D. taking the kaleidoscope apart

In Your Own Words

5. Could any of the steps in this process happen in a different order? Explain your answer.

_____

_____

_____

On Your Own!

Read this passage. Answer the questions that follow it.

I always pass the same places on my way to school in the morning. Sometimes I even see the same people. I like it when it happens the same way each day, because it gives me the feeling that the day will turn out to be exceptional.

First, I leave my house and walk down the street. We live on a busy street, so I stay on the sidewalk and make sure to check for traffic before crossing. Then I walk by a preschool and wave to the teachers outside. They're really nice.

Next, I pass the gym. My dad goes there in the morning before work. Some days, he walks out of the gym to catch the bus to work just as I pass by. That's always great, because then we get to chat for a minute or two before his bus comes.

Then I walk by the corner store. Mr. Sanchez, the store's owner, is sometimes leaning out the window. He always waves to me. Some days I stop in for a quick snack and use up most of my lunch money. I try not to do that too often!

Finally, I get to school! I like to arrive at school at the same time as my best friend's bus. I wait for him to get off the bus, so we can walk into school together.

---

1. Where does the narrator go **first**?

   A. into his house

   B. onto the sidewalk

   C. the preschool

   D. the gym

2. What is the **first** place the narrator passes?

   A. the preschool

   B. the gym

   C. the bus stop

   D. the corner store

3. What place does the narrator pass by right **after** he passes by the preschool?

   A. the corner store

   B. his school

   C. the gym

   D. his friend's bus stop

4. The narrator passes by the corner store right **after** seeing

   A. the preschool teachers

   B. Mr. Sanchez

   C. his mother

   D. his dad

5. What is the narrator's final destination?

   A. the preschool

   B. his school

   C. his house

   D. the corner store

6. What is the **last** thing the narrator does in this passage?

   A. walk to the gym with his dad

   B. buy a snack at the corner store

   C. wait for his friend at the bus

   D. wave to the preschool teachers

Write It Out   Use the passage to help you write brief answers to the questions below.

7. Why is it important that this passage is written in chronological order? What would happen if the events were written in a different order?

   _____

   _____

   _____

   _____

   _____

WORDS TO KNOW Three main types of literature are fiction, poetry, and drama. **Fiction** is any story about imaginary people and events. **Poetry** has stanzas and lines that may rhyme. **Drama** is divided into acts and scenes, and has dialogue and stage directions. In drama, the name of the character speaking is set off from the text, and the dialogue follows.

Review It! Read this passage. Use the Hint to help you determine the form of writing it is.

CAT: Meow! Give me back my string.
DOG: *[running away]* Come and get it!

> **Hint** Look at the words, or dialogue, the characters say. What type of literature presents dialogue in this way?

Try It! Read this passage. <u>Underline</u> clues that help you determine the type of literature it is.

Act 2, Scene 3: *Trevor enters from stage right. The other characters are seated in the hotel lobby.*

MORTIE: What's this all about, Trevor? We all want to leave the hotel.

TREVOR: Well, I need you all here. One of you stole Madam Poodle's necklace.

MISS PLACE: It couldn't have been me. I was on stage all evening.

[Miss Place dabs her face with a tissue to remove her heavy stage makeup.]

BUCK: *[quietly]* You weren't there the whole time.

[Miss Place glances angrily at Buck. She motions for him to be quiet.]

TREVOR: You're right, Buck. Where were you during intermission, Miss Place?

MISS PLACE: I went to my room for some water. I have to protect my voice!

TREVOR: Interesting! Guess what I found outside Madam Poodle's suite?

BUCK: A water bottle with a red lipstick mark on it!

Now, use the passage to answer the questions on the following page.

1. This passage can be described as

    A. a short story

    B. a drama

    C. a poem

    D. an essay

2. How is this passage arranged?

    A. by main idea and details

    B. in paragraphs and sentences

    C. in lines and stanzas

    D. in acts and scenes

    2.
    Look at the very first line of text in the passage. What does it tell you?

3. How are the sentences written?

    A. as dialogue

    B. as rhymes

    C. by topic

    D. by cause and effect

    3.
    What comes at the beginning of each group of sentences? Why?

4. Why are some words in *italic* print?

    A. They are dialogue.

    B. They are stage directions.

    C. They are to be read with emphasis.

    D. They answer audience questions.

In Your Own Words

5. What is the purpose of the stage directions?

    _____

    _____

    _____

    _____

    5.
    What information do stage directions give to people reading or performing a play?

Reading Literature

On Your Own!

Read this passage. Answer the questions that follow it.

The Ocean Waves to Me

At times you softly pat the shore
As if to reach for more and more,
And cover the sand in your salty embrace
As you come in and out with a steady pace.

At times you strike with force and power,
Attacking the shore for hour upon hour.
Your angry waves crashing into the sand,
Pummeling it heavily with your watery hand.

The times I like best—when you roll with grace,
Tumbling forward at a whimsical pace.
Rising and falling, dancing and twirling,
Stretching up high and suddenly curling.

1. **What type of passage is this?**

   A. poem

   B. short story

   C. play

   D. article

2. **How are the sentences arranged?**

   A. in acts

   B. in scenes

   C. in paragraphs

   D. in stanzas

3. How are the words arranged?

   A. The last words in the first and third lines rhyme.

   B. The last words in each pair of lines rhyme.

   C. All the lines end with the same sound.

   D. The first words in each line rhyme.

4. Why are the words arranged as they are?

   A. Words often rhyme in poems.

   B. Words often rhyme in drama.

   C. Words often rhyme in articles.

   D. Words often rhyme in stories.

5. Which is **not** a reason the sentences are arranged as they are?

   A. It is the typical way poems are written.

   B. It helps the author get the meaning across.

   C. It is a logical way to organize the information.

   D. It is the way a description is written.

6. In the last stanza, the poet describes the waves as

   A. angry attackers

   B. salty embraces

   C. twirling dancers

   D. clumsy tumblers

Write It Out Use the passage to write a brief answer to the question below.

7. What type of activity does the author describe in the second stanza?

_____

_____

_____

_____

Reading Literature

WORDS TO KNOW   **Plot**   the series of events that take place in a story. Plot consists of a conflict, or problem; a climax, or turning point; and a resolution of the conflict.

Review It!

Read these sentences. Use the Hint to help you determine the problem that will be solved by the end of the story.

The shepherd and his dog were frantic. Two sheep were missing from the flock. To make things worse, the shepherd was sure he heard a wolf in the distance.

> **Hint**   Two sheep are missing and a wolf is nearby. What problem does this cause for the shepherd?

Try It!

Read this passage. As you read, <u>underline</u> sentences that describe plot events.

(1) Gabby stood at the pool's edge with goose bumps on her arms and legs. She wasn't wet or cold, just nervous. She had to win this race. Gabby took deep breaths and saw herself making the perfect stroke. She was trying to ignore Mia, the former champion, standing next to her.

(2) Gabby put on her goggles and placed her toes on the edge of the platform. She was in position to dive. The starting gun rang and seemed to push her body into the water.

(3) When she reached the other side of the pool, she saw Mia next to her. Gabby pushed off for her last lap, determined to gain a stroke. Her hands sliced the water. As she touched the edge, she looked to her right. Mia touched the edge seconds later. Gabby shook Mia's hand and then headed to the winner's podium.

Now, use the passage to answer the questions on the following page.

Reading Literature

1. The conflict in this story in this story is between

   A. Gabby and the water

   B. Gabby and her coach

   C. Gabby and Mia

   D. Gabby and the swim team

2. What is Gabby's problem in the story?

   A. She wants to win the race.

   B. She thinks Mia may cheat in the race.

   C. She is afraid of swimming.

   D. She is recovering from an injury.

   > **2.**
   > What is Gabby thinking about nervously?

3. The story reaches its climax

   A. when Gabby puts on her goggles

   B. when Gabby dives into the water

   C. when Gabby looks up and sees that she and Mia are tied

   D. when Gabby walks to the winner's podium after the race

   > **3.**
   > What event signals that the story action may change?

4. How do you know that the resolution has been reached?

   A. Gabby stands at the edge of the pool.

   B. Gabby pushes off for the last lap.

   C. Gabby dives into the pool.

   D. Gabby finishes seconds ahead of Mia.

In Your Own Words

5. Describe how the conflict is solved by the end of the story.

   > **5.**
   > How and when is Gabby's problem solved?

   _____

   _____

   _____

   _____

Reading Literature

On Your Own!

Read this passage. Answer the questions that follow it.

Rob and Drew had been best friends since second grade. They were inseparable, even in competition. No matter what event they competed in, Drew won and Rob took second place. So when Drew suggested that they try indoor climbing at the new climbing gym, Rob hesitantly agreed.

On the day of the climb, the boys put on their safety gear and stared up at the large wall above them. The climb started out smoothly. Both boys found strongholds for their feet and steadily pushed themselves up. With his usual speed, Drew easily took the lead and was soon ahead of Rob.

About halfway up, the wall became more difficult. Rob smiled. He knew that Drew had speed, but he had endurance. "This could be my chance," he thought as he pulled himself even with Drew. The friends smiled, knowing a friendly challenge was on!

They were just a few feet from the top. As Rob stretched to the next hold, he heard a scraping noise and glanced down to see Drew lose his footing. Drew held tight to the hold with his fingers as his feet found their place. Assured that his friend was safe, Rob cleared the wall's top. Then he reached down to help his friend up and over the edge. They both smiled.

1. In this story, the conflict is between

   A. the boys and the other teams

   B. the boys and the wall

   C. Rob and the wall

   D. Rob and Drew

2. What is Rob's problem?

   A. He is afraid of heights.

   B. Drew always wins.

   C. He slips while climbing.

   D. He thinks Drew is playing unfair.

3. Why is the third paragraph important to the story?

  A. It shows the boys can climb high.

  B. It describes an important change of events.

  C. It shows that Rob wants Drew to fall.

  D. It describes how Rob can stretch easily.

4. Which event signals a possible big change in the story's outcome?

  A. Drew slips, and Rob keeps climbing.

  B. Rob helps Drew over the top of the wall.

  C. Drew invites Rob to the climbing wall.

  D. The boys gather the gear and start the climb.

5. The fourth paragraph shows

  A. how Rob's problem gets bigger

  B. how the boys stop being friends

  C. how the main conflict is solved

  D. how much Drew needs Rob

6. The story's conflict is solved when

  A. Drew helps Rob over the edge of the wall

  B. the boys decide climbing is too dangerous and quit

  C. Rob and Drew decide to work as a team and finish together

  D. Rob reaches the top first

Write It Out   Use the story to help you write a brief answer to the question below.

7. What is another ending for this story? Tell how the conflict might be solved differently.

_____

_____

_____

_____

_____

Reading Literature

Reading Literature

| WORDS TO KNOW | **Setting** where and when a story takes place |

Review It!
Read these sentences. Use the Hint to help you determine the setting.

All the other players had left, but Jamal sat on the wooden bench staring at his locker. He still had his uniform and basketball shoes on. He couldn't get over the team's loss.

> **Hint** The author doesn't tell the setting, but includes details such as a wooden bench, locker, uniform, and basketball shoes to help you picture the setting.

Try It!
Read this passage. As you read, <u>underline</u> words that give you clues about when and where the story takes place.

(1) Awakened by the sound of the radio newscast coming from the kitchen, Lauren glanced at the calendar through sleepy eyes. Normally, she'd have run downstairs yelling, "It's my birthday!" Life was different now that her father was flying bombers in Europe.

(2) She went downstairs for breakfast. Mother had made eggs and toast. Lauren missed having butter on her toast. Like sugar and gasoline, butter was rationed. With troops fighting the war, people at home had restrictions on what they could buy.

(3) Pete and Sarah dashed in for breakfast with wide grins on their faces. After the children were seated, their mother placed a beautifully frosted cake on the table. Mother must have saved her sugar ration cards for two months to be able to make that! Pete and Sarah each handed Lauren packages that they had wrapped in old newspaper. Best of all, there was a letter from her father! Maybe today would be better than she thought.

Now, use the passage to answer the questions on the following page.

1. Where does the story take place?

   A. at Lauren's school

   B. at Lauren's house

   C. on the war front

   D. in Europe

2. What time of day does the story take place?

   A. morning

   B. lunchtime

   C. after school

   D. nighttime

2.

Why is Lauren going downstairs?

3. The story most likely takes place during

   A. pioneer days

   B. the Civil War

   C. the 1940s

   D. the future

3.

Are bombers and rationing specific to a certain time period?

4. Which sentence **best** helps you identify the time period in which the story takes place?

   A. "...Lauren glanced at the calendar through sleepy eyes."

   B. "Mother must have saved her sugar ration cards for two months to be able to make that!"

   C. "...mother placed a beautifully frosted cake on the table."

   D. "Maybe today would be better than she thought."

In Your Own Words

5. How might this story be different if it took place today?

   _____

   _____

   _____

5.

What details of Lauren's birthday celebration would be different?

Reading Literature

On Your Own!

Read this passage. Answer the questions that follow it.

Tobias was tired, but excited too. Pa had never asked him to help in the fields before. Tobias usually spent the morning caring for the animals and cutting wood. Times had not been easy since they loaded the covered wagon and began their journey to the far West.

At their old home, winter had meant a welcome relief from chores. But now, whenever there was a break in the snow, Pa toiled hard to get the field ready to plant in the spring. Clearing fields was hard work. This morning Tobias helped Pa clear around the stumps. Then they tied ropes around the stumps and attached them to Betsy, their mule. Tobias urged Betsy to pull. As Betsy tugged on the stump, Pa cut the roots with an ax until the stump was removed from the ground.

Tobias sat and looked around at the pile of stumps. He opened up the tin pail that Ma had packed earlier this morning. He gobbled up the cornbread and salted meat. Breakfast seemed so long ago. He couldn't wait to taste the hot stew Ma would have bubbling on the fire for supper.

Tobias had blisters forming from his work cutting the stumps. Pa dipped his handkerchief in cold water and placed it around Tobias's sore hands. Tobias was ready to work again. Pa said that with Tobias's help, the ground would be cleared by March. Tobias had never felt so proud.

---

1. Where does this story take place?

   A. in a swamp

   B. at home on a prairie

   C. on a farm

   D. in a barn near Tobias's house

2. What time of day does the story take place?

   A. before breakfast

   B. before lunchtime

   C. after dinner

   D. after bedtime

3. What paragraph **best** helped you to determine the time of day when the story takes place?

    A. first paragraph

    B. second paragraph

    C. third paragraph

    D. last paragraph

4. In which part of the country is the farm?

    A. the North

    B. the South

    C. the East

    D. the West

5. In what time period does the story take place?

    A. American Revolution

    B. pioneer days

    C. World War II

    D. the present

6. Which clue **best** helped you to determine the time period?

    A. "... caring for the animals and cutting wood."

    B. "Pa toiled hard to get the field ready to plant in the spring."

    C. "Pa cut the roots with an ax ..."

    D. "... the hot stew Ma would have bubbling on the fire for supper."

Write It Out   Use the story to help you write a brief answer to the question below.

7. How would Tobias's day be different if the story were set in a city?

_____

_____

_____

_____

_____

Reading Literature

Characters the people or animals about whom a story is told. Readers learn about characters from what they say, do, and think.

 **Review It!** Read these sentences. Use the Hint to determine how the character is feeling.

Aiden hid his face as he tried to sneak by the group of kids on his way to detention. He heard one of them whisper, "Aiden is the one who cheated? I can't believe it!" Aiden's shoulders slumped.

> **Hint** What does Aiden's behavior tell you about his feelings?

Reading Literature

Try It! Read this passage. As you read, <u>circle</u> the name of the main character. <u>Underline</u> sentences that give you information about his or her thoughts, feelings, and actions.

(1) Mrs. Elias begins the history lesson. Cameron leans over and loudly whispers, "Can I borrow a pencil?" Giving him an annoyed look, Shontal sighs. She passes him a new pencil.

(2) Shontal realizes that Mrs. Elias is explaining the details of their history project. Mrs. Elias writes the due date on the board. Shontal's heart starts to race and her palms get sweaty. "Only two days to get it done," Shontal says to herself, panicking.

(3) She takes out her planner and takes a deep breath. "Let's see. If I reschedule my piano lesson and the movies, I should have enough time." She starts to feel relieved. Then she begins mapping out her plans.

Now, use the passage to answer the questions on the following page.

1. Who is the main character?

   A. Cameron

   B. Mrs. Elias

   C. the principal

   D. Shontal

2. How does Shontal feel about Cameron's request?

   A. irritated

   B. surprised

   C. pleased

   D. anxious

2.

What does Shontal do after Cameron asks for a pencil?

3. Why does Shontal panic in paragraph 2?

   A. She forgot to do her homework assignment.

   B. Mrs. Elias has called her to the front of the class.

   C. She forgot a book that she needs for the project.

   D. She is worried that she won't have enough time to finish the project.

3.

How does Shontal react as she reads the date on the board?

4. Which **best** describes Shontal's behavior in paragraph 3?

   A. She ignores a problem.

   B. She loses hope.

   C. She isn't discouraged for long.

   D. She is annoyed.

In Your Own Words

5. How does the author help you understand Shontal's character?

   _____

   _____

   _____

   _____

5.

How does the author describe Shontal's actions?

Reading Literature

On Your Own!

Read this passage. Answer the questions that follow it.

The jungle animals had called a meeting. Lion presided, since the animals looked to him for leadership. All the animals, except one, were in attendance.

Monkey spoke first. "I've had it! Today he took all of my bananas." Monkey's face was red as he paced excitedly, waving his hands in the air.

"That explains what happened to me," interrupted timid Zebra. "While I was walking, I slipped on a pile of banana peels and sprained my hoof. Why does he pick on me?"

Just then Spider walked by. "Hmm . . . a meeting. Perhaps I should listen in."

Lion roared loudly. "Quiet! We can't all speak at once. I know that you are upset, but does anyone have proof that it was Spider?"

"You know we don't!" yelled Snake, who had a bandage on his tail from one of Spider's tricks.

Lion listened thoughtfully. He suspected the animals were right, but he didn't want to accuse Spider unjustly. "We need to catch Spider in the act. Then we can punish him."

"Yes, but how?" wailed Zebra. "He's gotten away with things before."

"They won't catch me," muttered Spider as he listened. "I need a plan of my own," he thought as a new scheme began to run through his head.

1. Which character is the trickster?

    A. Monkey

    B. Zebra

    C. Spider

    D. Snake

2. Monkey **most likely** feels

    A. calm

    B. happy

    C. angry

    D. sad

3. Which word **best** describes Lion?

   A. greedy

   B. fair

   C. critical

   D. careless

4. Which of the following **best** describes Spider's behavior in the fourth paragraph?

   A. sneaky

   B. mean

   C. helpful

   D. kind

5. How can Zebra's feelings be described?

   A. afraid

   B. cheerful

   C. angry

   D. discouraged

6. Which **best** describes Spider's character?

   A. easily gets confused

   B. takes the lead

   C. likes to play tricks

   D. enjoys helping others

Write It Out Complete the chart to show how you learn about Spider's character.

7.

Source	What you learn
what Spider says	
what Spider does	
what Spider thinks	

| WORDS TO KNOW | **Theme** the central idea or meaning of a story; a lesson about life |

 **Read these sentences. Use the Hint to determine the theme.**

As Mother Rabbit looked tearfully at the damage the flood had done to her burrow, she grabbed her little bunnies close to her. She realized the flood had not destroyed what was most important.

> **Hint**   What is most important to Mother Rabbit?

 **Read this passage. As you read, <u>underline</u> sentences that help to identify the theme.**

(1) "Pop quiz!" announced Mr. Ruiz. "Take out a sheet of paper."

(2) While everyone else reacted with shock, David hung his head. He couldn't look up. He was thinking about what happened yesterday.

(3) Yesterday, when he was at the board, David noticed a sticky note in Mr. Ruiz's lesson plan. It said, "POP QUIZ tomorrow—science." So that night, David had studied hard for the test. Then he'd hardly slept because he felt so guilty and didn't know what to do. He knew Mr. Ruiz had always trusted him.

(4) The rest of the day, David walked around feeling sick inside. Finally, he went back to Mr. Ruiz's room and told him the whole story. Mr. Ruiz thanked him for telling the truth. He told David that he would have to do a special project to make up for the pop quiz. Even though it meant more work, David couldn't help smiling.

Now, use the passage to answer the questions on the following page.

1. What is the theme of this passage?

   A. People who work hard are rewarded.

   B. Honesty has its own rewards.

   C. You have to take care of yourself.

   D. Treat others kindly.

2. Which paragraph **best** supports the theme?

   A. paragraph 1

   B. paragraph 2

   C. paragraph 3

   D. paragraph 4

2.
Which paragraph reveals the lesson David learned?

3. How do you think the author feels about honesty?

   A. He thinks being honest makes you feel good.

   B. He thinks there are times when telling the truth is harmful.

   C. He thinks telling a little lie can get you out of trouble.

   D. He thinks being honest can get you into trouble.

3.
What happens when David tells the truth?

4. Which title would **best** express the theme of the story?

   A. "David Tells the Truth"

   B. "Always Do Your Best"

   C. "How to Get an A"

   D. "Mr. Ruiz Gets Mad"

In Your Own Words

5. How might this story be different if the theme were "Do whatever you can to win"?

   _____

   _____

   _____

   _____

5.
How would David feel and behave if he only wanted to get a high grade on the quiz?

Reading Literature

On Your Own!   Read this passage. Answer the questions that follow it.

Everyone said Ellie couldn't do it. Even her mom had discouraged her. "That's an awfully big job, Ellie," she'd said. "Why don't you pick another project? Maybe you can volunteer at the hospital or the library. They always need help."

But Ellie felt up to the challenge. Every day after school and on Saturdays, she spent her time at the empty lot down the block from her family's apartment. Sometimes she got discouraged and was tempted to think the job would never get done. The lot had been ignored for years. There were huge piles of soda bottles and newspapers to prove it. No one else seemed to see what the lot had to offer. Someone had even dumped all of their trash over the fence and crushed her first batch of flowers.

It was hard facing the mess almost every day. Whenever she felt sad or doubted herself, Ellie remembered what her Nana had said: "You can move a mountain, if only you believe you can." Ellie knew Nana was right. She had to finish her work in the empty lot.

Now Ellie looked around the beautiful flower garden. Only weeks earlier it had been a messy, garbage-filled lot. "I did it!" she said proudly.

1. What is the theme of this story?

   A. It is important to give back to your community.

   B. Believe in yourself, and you will succeed.

   C. Always listen to your parents.

   D. It is good to help others who are in need.

2. Which paragraph **best** supports the theme?

   A. first paragraph

   B. second paragraph

   C. third paragraph

   D. last paragraph

3. Ellie's actions tell us that she

   A. only cares about herself

   B. has a lot in common with Nana

   C. thinks that everyone should agree with her

   D. only wants to please her parents

4. After someone throws garbage into the lot and ruins her flowers, Ellie

   A. decides to give up on the project

   B. realizes that nobody notices her hard work

   C. is disappointed, but stays focused

   D. decides to leave the trash in the lot

5. What does the author want readers to understand about children?

   A. They can do more than people think.

   B. They need constant supervision.

   C. They can be thoughtful and caring.

   D. They should always respect adults.

6. Which title would **best** express the theme of the story?

   A. "From Trash to Treasure"

   B. "Ellie Believes"

   C. "How to Clean Up Your Neighborhood"

   D. "Flowers Aplenty"

Write It Out   Use the story to write a brief answer to the question below.

7. How would the story be different if the theme were "Working as a team accomplishes more"?

_____

_____

_____

_____

_____

WORDS TO KNOW

Rhyme   when words end with the same sound

Rhythm   the use of stressed and unstressed syllables to create a beat. The pattern of rhythm in a poem is called "meter."

Review It!

Read these lines aloud. Use the Hint to determine the rhythm.

Tiny babe without a peep,
Snuggled in the crib to sleep.

> **Hint**   Listen to the syllables you stress, or emphasize, as you read. This is the poem's rhythm. There are four stressed syllables in each line. This is its meter.

Try It!

Read this passage. As you read, <u>underline</u> the stressed syllables.

(1)   Little Robin Redbreast sat upon a tree,

(2)   Up went Kitty then down went he;

(3)   Down came Kitty and away Robin ran;

(4)   Said little Robin Redbreast, "Catch me if you can."

(5)   Little Robin Redbreast jumped upon a wall,

(6)   Kitty jumped after him and almost had a fall;

(7)   Robin chirped and sang, and what did Kitty say?

(8)   Kitty said, "Meow!" and Robin jumped away.

Now, use the passage to answer the questions on the following page.

Reading Literature

1. You know this passage is an example of poetry because

   A. it has stanzas and rhyming lines

   B. it is organized in paragraphs

   C. it features animal characters

   D. it is amusing

2. Which word in line 1 does **not** have a stressed syllable?

   A. Little   C. upon

   B. Redbreast   D. tree

3. Which statement **best** describes the rhyming structure of the poem?

   A. The last words in the first and third lines rhyme.

   B. The last words in every two lines rhyme.

   C. All the lines end with the same exact sound.

   D. The first words in each line rhyme.

4. How many stressed syllables are there in each line of the poem?

   A. 4   C. 6

   B. 5   D. 8

In Your Own Words

5. What does the poem describe?

   _____

   _____

   _____

   _____

Ask Yourself

2. When you read the poem aloud, which syllables are emphasized? Which ones are not?

3. Which lines end with the same sounds?

5. What story does the poem tell?

Reading Literature

On Your Own!

Read this passage. Answer the questions that follow it.

To My Puppy

1 Tiny, brown, and sweet,
2 Calmly lying at my feet,
3 You are adorable!

4 Only moments before,
5 When I came through the door,
6 You looked guilty!

7 You chewed my shoe,
8 The couch and rug, too.
9 You are a destroyer!

10 Man's best friend?
11 Loyal to the end?
12 You will learn!

1. What type of writing is this passage?

   A. informational article
   B. journal entry
   C. poem
   D. short story

2. What word in the passage rhymes with "shoe"?

   A. chewed
   B. destroyer
   C. too
   D. rug

3. Which word in the passage rhymes with "door"?

   A. before

   B. when

   C. through

   D. you

4. Which word in line 2 does **not** have a stressed syllable?

   A. calmly

   B. lying

   C. at

   D. my

5. Which describes the rhyming structure of each stanza?

   A. All the lines end with the same sound.

   B. The first words in each line rhyme.

   C. The last words in the first and third lines rhyme.

   D. The last words in the first and second lines rhyme.

6. How many stressed syllables does each line of the last stanza contain?

   A. 3

   B. 5

   C. 4

   D. 2

Write It Out   Use the passage to help you write a brief answer to the question below.

7. What story does the writer of this passage tell?

   _____

   _____

   _____

   _____

LESSON 21 Simile

 **Simile** a comparison of two unlike things using the words *like* or *as*

Review It! Read this sentence. Use the Hint to find the simile.

John jumped like a rabbit when the school bell rang.

> **Hint** Think about what is being compared. Here, the word *like* signals that a simile is being used.

Try It! Read this passage. As you read, <u>underline</u> the words *like* or *as* to help you locate the similes.

1   On Tuesday, Lake Middle School held its field day. The last event was the obstacle course. The coach blew the whistle, and the kids took off like charging bulls. Katie hopped through each tire, as quick as a rabbit. Cameron and Riley were close behind her, while Anna practically walked.

2   At the next obstacle, Katie stumbled on the beam but swung quickly across the mud puddle. Cameron was as steady as a rock on the beam, but it took him two tries to swing across the puddle. To Anna, still trailing behind, the ropes were like prison bars keeping her from going farther.

3   At the end, Riley scurried through the tunnels to take the lead. They crossed the finish line with Riley in first, then Katie in second, and Cameron in third. Anna came in last. She might have been as slow as a snail, but she was happy to finish the race.

Now, use the passage to answer the questions on the following page.

Reading Literature

1. **What is the simile in this sentence?**

   To Anna, still trailing behind, the ropes were like prison bars keeping her from going farther.

   A. "To Anna"   **C.** "the ropes were like prison bars"

   B. "still trailing behind"   **D.** "keeping her from going farther"

2. **The author compares the ropes to prison bars to show that**

   A. they are very scary

   B. they are made of metal

   C. there are many in a row

   D. they arc holding the runner back

> 2.
> Think about what Anna is trying to do. What do prison bars do?

3. **Which sentence from the passage includes a simile?**

   A. "On Tuesday, Lake Middle School held its field day."

   B. "The last event was the obstacle course."

   C. "...the kids took off like charging bulls."

   D. "...Riley scurried through the tunnels to take the lead."

4. **What simile does the author use to describe Cameron in paragraph 2?**

   A. as quick as a rabbit   **C.** as steady as a rock

   B. as slow as a snail   **D.** as strong as a bull

> 4.
> How was Cameron moving on the beam?

In Your Own Words

5. **Write a simile to describe Riley's movement through the tunnels.**

   _____

   _____

   _____

   _____

> 5.
> What is something that scurries?

Reading Literature

Read this passage. Answer the questions that follow it.

Fido was as gentle as a lamb, which is why nobody could understand why I was trembling. I'm terrified of dogs. When I see a dog, I run like my life depends on it. Imagine my dismay when my scout troop decided to volunteer at the animal shelter.

It started two years ago. My brother and I had been fighting like cats and dogs all morning. Mom got tired of it and sent us to the park. When we got there, I saw a dog. I reached out my hand to pet it, and it exploded like a volcano, growling and nipping me several times. Since then, I haven't been able to get near a dog without shaking.

Seeing my fear, the workers at the shelter assigned me the job of organizing the leashes. They were heaped on the floor like a big pile of spaghetti. I untangled them and hung them up. One of the workers talked to me. He suggested that I might be able to overcome my fear by breathing deeply.

I walked toward a small dog lying in its cage. I nervously approached the cage, stopping every few steps to take some deep breaths. I reached out my hand toward the cage, concentrating on my breathing. Finally, I was able to stand right next to the cage. The breathing technique was working like a dream.

Reading Literature

1. **What is the simile in this sentence?**

   Fido was as gentle as a lamb, which is why nobody could understand why I was trembling.

   A. "Fido was as gentle as a lamb"

   B. "which is why nobody"

   C. "could understand why"

   D. "I was trembling"

2. **Which sentence from the passage includes a simile?**

   A. "When I see a dog, I run like my life depends on it."

   B. "My brother and I had been fighting like cats and dogs all morning."

   C. "Since that day, I have not been able to get near a dog without shaking."

   D. "I reached out my hand toward the cage, concentrating on my breathing."

3. To what does the narrator compare the dog in paragraph 2?

   A. a lamb

   B. spaghetti

   C. a volcano

   D. a cat

4. What is the narrator saying about the leashes when he compares them to spaghetti?

   A. They have sauce on them.

   B. They are long and wet.

   C. They are twisted and tangled.

   D. They are hanging in straight lines.

5. Which simile **best** describes how the narrator approached the dog's cage?

   A. as quickly as a fox

   B. as timidly as a kitten

   C. as carefully as an acrobat

   D. as playfully as a puppy

6. When the narrator says the breathing technique is "working like a dream" he **most likely** means

   A. he imagined the whole thing

   B. he wished it hadn't happened

   C. it was all a dream

   D. it was successful

Write It Out Use the story to help you write a brief answer to the question below.

7. In the last paragraph, the narrator says, "I walked toward a small dog lying in its cage." What simile could you use to describe the dog? Rewrite the sentence using a simile.

   _____

   _____

   _____

   _____

Reading Literature

LESSON 22 Metaphor

WORDS TO KNOW | **Metaphor**   a direct comparison of two things without using the words *like* or *as*

Review It!   Read this sentence. Use the Hint to find the metaphor.

The books were rocks in his backpack, weighing him down.

> **Hint**   To what are the books being compared? Remember, the comparison isn't meant to be taken literally.

Try It!   Read this passage. As you read, <u>underline</u> the metaphors you recognize.

(1)   *Yesterday, I interviewed Alex Smith, a giant in the field of music, to learn about his career. Here are some of the questions I asked him.*

(2)   *How did you get started in music?* Music has always been important in my life. I banged on pots when I was little. I began violin lessons when I was just a sprout. I took piano lessons from my mom when I turned four.

(3)   *Was your a mom a musician, as well?* Yes, she trained to be a concert pianist. She taught piano lessons at our house. She was the sunshine of my life growing up. She always encouraged me in my music.

(4)   *What kinds of music do you like best?* When my life is a storm of activity, I like listening to jazz. In calmer times, I prefer classical. But really, I enjoy all of it. Music is a special language. It speaks to everyone.

Now, use the passage to answer the questions on the following page.

1. Which sentence is a metaphor?

   A. "Yesterday, I interviewed Alex Smith . . ."

   B. ". . . I interviewed Alex Smith, a giant in the field of music . . ."

   C. "Was your mom a musician, as well?"

   D. "She taught piano lessons at our house."

1.
What is the writer comparing Alex Smith to in this paragraph?

2. Which sentence in paragraph 2 contains a metaphor?

   A. "Music has always been important in my life."

   B. "I banged on pots when I was little."

   C. "I began taking violin lessons when I was just a sprout."

   D. "I took piano lessons from my mom when I turned four."

3. In paragraph 3, when Smith says his mom "was the sunshine of my life," he means

   A. she made sure he could see his music

   B. she brought joy into his life

   C. she took good care of him

   D. she sang songs to him

4. In paragraph 4, what does Smith mean when he says, "Music is a special language"?

   A. Music is older than many languages.

   B. Music has an unusual alphabet.

   C. Music can be understood only if you study it.

   D. Music is a form of communication.

4.
How does knowing the purpose of language help you answer this question?

In Your Own Words

5. In your own words, explain what Smith means when he says his life is "a storm of activity."

5.
Think about what a storm is like. How could Smith's life be like a storm?

_____

_____

_____

On Your Own!

Read this passage. Answer the questions that follow it.

As we went to bed on April 17, 1906, neither I nor the other people in San Francisco had any idea of what was to come. I awoke abruptly at 5:12 A.M. My bed was a bucking bronco, shaking violently in all directions. As I woke from a sound sleep, it took several seconds for me to realize that this was an earthquake. My quiet life was now a terrifying nightmare.

I was a statue, frozen in fear until the rumbling ended. As soon as it stopped, I cautiously left my room. My mother came out of the bedroom with my sister. Together, we all went out into the street. We looked around. The ground was a blanket of debris, littered with shattered glass, bricks from toppled buildings, and fallen trees. At first everyone stood still in shocked disbelief. Then suddenly they were a whirlwind of movement. Within minutes the streets became a steady flood of people moving up the hill toward us.

That's when we noticed the smoke coming from downtown. Huge fires had ignited after the earthquake and were spreading quickly. My father rushed us inside, and we began packing our bags. We were lucky; we had a horse and wagon that could carry us safely out of the city.

---

1. **Which sentence from the first paragraph contains a metaphor?**

    A. "I awoke abruptly at 5:12 A.M."

    B. "...it took several seconds for me to realize that this was an earthquake."

    C. "...neither I nor the other people of San Francisco had any idea of what was to come."

    D. "My quiet life was now a terrifying nightmare."

2. **When the narrator says "My bed was a bucking bronco . . ." she means**

    A. she had a bed shaped like a horse

    B. her room had a western theme

    C. her bed was bumping and moving all around

    D. she bought her bed from a cowboy

3. Which sentence from the passage contains a metaphor?

   A. "I was a statue, frozen in fear until the rumbling ended."

   B. "As soon as it stopped, I cautiously left my room."

   C. "My mother came out of the bedroom with my sister."

   D. "Together, we all went out into the street."

4. What does the narrator mean when she says, "The ground was a blanket of debris . . ."?

   A. The ground was very warm.

   B. The ground was covered with glass and bricks.

   C. The ground was smooth.

   D. The ground was covered with large pieces of cloth.

5. What does the narrator mean when she says the streets were "a steady flood of people . . ."?

   A. There was water flooding everywhere.

   B. A river was flowing up the hill.

   C. The streets were crowded with people.

   D. A few people were in the streets.

6. Which sentence from the passage contains a metaphor?

   A. "Then suddenly they were a whirlwind of movement."

   B. "That's when we noticed the smoke coming from downtown."

   C. "Huge fires had ignited after the earthquake and were spreading quickly."

   D. "My father rushed us inside, and we began packing our bags."

Reading Literature

Write It Out   Use the passage to help you write a brief answer to the question below.

7. In the last paragraph, the narrator says, "Huge fires had ignited after the earthquake and were spreading quickly." What metaphor could you use to describe the fires? Rewrite the sentence using a metaphor.

   _____

   _____

   _____

   _____

WORDS TO KNOW **Personification** giving human qualities to something that is not human, like an animal or object

---

Review It!

Read this sentence. Use the Hint to identify the example of personification.

The chocolate cake called my name from across the room.

Hint A cake can't really talk, of course. The use of personification points to the cake's strong appeal.

Try It!

Read this passage. As you read, <u>underline</u> examples of personification.

1 Every year my family hikes up Long Pass Trail. We begin before dawn. Although my brother complains that it's not light yet, I love how the darkness hugs me. I appreciate how quiet nature is before it wakes up. As we walk up the mountain, the sun peeks over the horizon. The sky turns from subtle pink to blazing orange.

2 The trail gets tougher by mid-morning. We all appreciate the light now. It warms us and helps us to see our way. The path grows steadily steeper, and rocks and tree roots make things more difficult. By lunch we are grateful to have reached a bubbling stream. We munch on trail mix and enjoy the scenery. Delicate pink and white flowers beg us to notice them as they sway in the wind. We take in as much natural beauty as we can before we begin the challenging trip back down.

Now, use the passage to answer the questions on the following page.

Reading Literature

1. Which phrase from the passage shows personification?

    A. "Although my brother complains . . ."

    B. "The path grows steadily steeper . . ."

    C. ". . . appreciate the light now."

    D. ". . . the darkness hugs me."

Ask Yourself

1.
What human characteristic does the darkness have?

2. In paragraph 1, what does the narrator mean by "the sun peeks over the horizon"?

    A. The sun rises.

    B. The sun is partially covered by a cloud.

    C. The sun looks out at the people.

    D. The sun goes behind the mountain.

3. Which sentence from the passage shows personification?

    A. "Every year my family hikes up Long Pass Trail."

    B. "I appreciate how quiet nature is before it wakes up."

    C. "The sky turns from subtle pink to blazing orange."

    D. "The trail gets tougher by mid-morning."

3.
In which sentence can something nonhuman do something that people do?

4. Which sentence from the passage shows personification?

    A. "We begin before dawn."

    B. "Delicate pink and white flowers beg us to notice them as they sway in the wind.

    C. "We munch on trail mix and enjoy the scenery."

    D. "We take in as much natural beauty as we can before we begin the challenging trip back down."

In Your Own Words

5. Write a sentence using personification to describe the trees that the family might see on the trail.

5.
What human qualities could you give the trees? What might a tree branch "do" or "say"?

_____

_____

Reading Literature

"Argh! This computer hates me! I can't believe it broke down again. And the night before my science project is due." Matt covered his face with his hands. "Maybe it's not that bad." He peeked through his fingers. Then the computer hiccupped and coughed. The screen went blank and was silent.

"Mom," Matt yelled. "Help!" The stairs creaked, alerting Matt that help was on the way.

"What's up?" Mom asked as she came into his room. Matt pointed to the blank screen. "This may be fixable," she said. "The guide book will tell us what to do."

Matt's mom narrowed the problem down to the power cord. Then she went into the garage and dug through a carton looking for a spare. "Why is that cord hiding from me?" she moaned. Finally, she found a spare cord and brought it to Matt. As she plugged in the computer using the new cord, she and Matt both held their breath. The computer blinked on. It gave a sigh.

"Mom! You're my hero." Matt laughed. With his computer humming along like new, Matt got back to his project.

---

1. Which sentence from the passage shows personification?

   A. "This computer hates me!"

   B. "I can't believe it broke down again."

   C. "Matt covered his face with his hands."

   D. "He peeked through his fingers."

2. Read this sentence from the passage.

   The stairs creaked, alerting Matt that help was on the way.

   What does this sentence mean?

   A. He has an alarm on the stairs.

   B. The stairs yell to him that his mom is coming.

   C. The creaking noise lets him know someone is walking upstairs.

   D. Mom tells him that she is coming.

3. Which sentence from the passage shows personification?

   A. "Then the computer hiccupped and coughed."

   B. "The screen went blank and was silent."

   C. "Matt pointed to the blank screen."

   D. "Matt's mom narrowed the problem down to the power cord."

4. Read this sentence from the passage.

   "Why is that cord hiding from me?" she moaned.

   What does this sentence mean?

   A. The cord does not want to be found.

   B. The cord is not in the garage at all.

   C. The cord is buried under other things.

   D. The cord does not work.

5. Which is **not** an example of personification?

   A. " 'Why is that cord hiding from me?' she moaned."

   B. "Matt laughed."

   C. "The computer blinked on."

   D. "It gave a sigh."

6. The author says the computer is "humming along like new" to show that

   A. Matt is listening to music on his computer

   B. Matt and his mom weren't able to fix the computer

   C. Matt's science project is about humming

   D. the computer is working perfectly now

Write It Out Use the passage to write a brief response to the prompt below.

7. In the fourth paragraph, the author says, "Finally, she found a spare cord." Rewrite the sentence using personification to describe the power cord.

   _____

   _____

   _____

WORDS TO KNOW	**Symbolism** a literary device that uses an object to represent a theme, idea, or emotion

Reading Literature

Review It!

Read these sentences. Use the Hint to determine what the dove symbolizes.

Tiger and Lion were fighting over who was king. A soft cooing stopped their argument as a dove flew gracefully across the sky. Distracted, Lion looked at Tiger and said, "Let's stop this silly argument."

> **Hint** What happens after the dove flies over? What idea does the dove represent?

Try It!

Read this passage. As you read, <u>underline</u> any symbols you see.

(1) Carmen lies on her bed, the darkness of the room pressing down on her. It feels as heavy as her memory of what happened at school today, when she fell off the stage during the talent show. The whole auditorium was silent. Then the laughing started. She hides her head under the safety of the blanket, pressing deeper into the blackness.

(2) There is a gentle rap at the door. "Go away!" Carmen moans. As the door opens, rays of light shine in from the hall, warming the room and begging her to open her eyes.

(3) "That was some move!" says Julia. Carmen peeks out from under the blanket and feels the warmth and light. "C'mon," Julia beckons her friend. "There's only one cure for a day like this, popcorn and a movie." As she drags Carmen into the bright light, a smile begins to form at the corners of Carmen's mouth.

Now, use the passage to answer the questions on the following page.

1. What symbol is used in paragraph 1?

    A. the stage   **C.** the darkness

    B. the blanket   **D.** a memory

2. The symbol in paragraph 1 represents

    A. Carmen's sadness

    B. Carmen's performance

    C. Carmen's room

    D. Carmen's school

    2.
    How is Carmen's mood described in the paragraph?

3. What symbol is used in paragraph 2?

    A. light   **C.** a smile

    B. friendship   **D.** a movie

4. What does the symbol in paragraph 2 represent?

    A. Julia's friendship

    B. a happier mood

    C. movies and popcorn

    D. a friend's searching

    4.
    How does Carmen's attitude change?

In Your Own Words

5. Imagine that Carmen had been waiting a long time for Julia to arrive. In that case, what symbol could be used to symbolize her impatience?

    5.
    What object might represent impatience?

    _____

    _____

    _____

    _____

Reading Literature

Reading Literature

It was easier to look outside than to look at the people in the room. So I stared at the dark, gray clouds. Not a ray of light could get through those clouds. A knot formed in my stomach as I waited for the principal to call my name. I was anxious. I had no idea what I would say. I wanted to protect my friend, but I didn't want to lie.

As Ms. White called my name, I dragged my feet slowly toward her office. Glancing out the window once more, I think I was hoping for a way to escape. Surprisingly, a ray of sunshine streamed through the clouds. "Tomas, I want to thank you for coming today." Was that a smile on her face? I wondered. "Miguel stopped by earlier and told me the whole story. He told me that you encouraged him to be honest and to admit what he had done."

I remained silent, still staring out the window. I wasn't sure what to say. I noticed a rainbow breaking through the clouds and washing the sky with color. "It took a lot of courage to stand up to your friend," said Ms. White. All I could stammer was a surprised, "Thank you, Ms. White." Then she walked me out of her office. I was still in shock. This definitely hadn't turned out as I had feared.

---

1. **What symbol is used in the first paragraph?**

   A. the room

   B. dark clouds

   C. a friend

   D. sunshine

2. **In the first paragraph, the weather symbolizes Tomas's**

   A. dread

   B. excitement

   C. anger

   D. frustration

3. What symbol is used in the second paragraph?

    A. the chair

    B. a smile

    C. a ray of sunshine

    D. a bird in flight

4. How does the weather give a hint to what comes next in the second paragraph?

    A. It shows the principal's anger.

    B. It shows Tomas's upcoming punishment.

    C. It shows that something bad is about to happen.

    D. It shows that things are about to get better.

5. What symbol is used in the third paragraph?

    A. a rainbow

    B. the window

    C. Ms. White

    D. the sky

6. How does the weather symbolize Tomas's mood in the third paragraph?

    A. The clouds show his bleak mood.

    B. The rainbow shows his hope that the situation is worked out.

    C. The clouds show that things are about to get worse.

    D. The rainbow shows that he has learned to tell the truth.

Write It Out   Use the story to help you write a brief answer to the question below.

7. Imagine that Tomas goes outside at the end of the story. What season might be described to symbolize Tomas's mood? Why?

    _____

    _____

    _____

Reading Literature

WORDS TO KNOW

Simple sentence   a group of words that has one subject and one predicate

Compound sentence   two or more simple sentences put together

Sentence fragment   an incomplete sentence. A sentence fragment is missing either a subject or a predicate.

Review It!

Read this sentence. Use the Hint to help you identify the subject and predicate.

The majestic emperor penguin slides down the snowy hill on its stomach.

> **Hint**   The subject tells who or what the sentence is about. This sentence is about a penguin. The predicate describes what the subject is doing. The penguin is sliding down a hill.

Try It!

Read this passage. As you read, circle the subjects and <u>underline</u> the predicates.

(1) Have you ever lost a tooth? Can you imagine losing teeth all the time? Our teeth fall out when we are children, but sharks lose and replace their teeth all the time. Sharks have many teeth. Sharks' teeth are sharp. Sharks' teeth are set in rows. When one tooth breaks, a tooth from the next row is ready to move into its place.

(2) Different kinds of sharks. Have different kinds of teeth. Some sharks catch small fish. Like the lemon fish. They have narrow teeth for stabbing the fish and eating them whole. Sharks, like the great white shark, hunt larger animals. They have teeth with jagged edges, like a knife, to tear the meat into pieces. Some sharks have both kinds of teeth, which allow them to both hold their prey and tear it.

Now, use the passage to answer the questions on the following page.

Editing

Ask Yourself

1. Read this sentence from the passage.

Can you imagine losing teeth all the time?

What kind of sentence is this?

A. simple sentence   **C.** sentence fragment

B. compound sentence   **D.** complex sentence

2. Read this sentence from the passage.

Our teeth fall out when we are children, but sharks lose and replace their teeth all the time.

What kind of sentence is this?

A. simple sentence   **C.** sentence fragment

B. compound sentence   **D.** complex sentence

2.
How many subjects and predicates does the sentence have?

3. Which of the following is **not** a complete sentence?

A. Have you ever lost a tooth?

B. Sharks' teeth are set in rows.

C. Different kinds of sharks.

D. When one tooth breaks, a tooth from the next row is ready to move into its place.

3.
Which answer choice is missing a subject or a predicate?

4. Choose the best way to combine this sentence and fragment.

Some sharks catch small fish. Like the lemon fish.

A. Some sharks catch small fish, like the lemon fish.

B. Some sharks catch small fish like the lemon fish.

C. Some sharks catch small fish and like the lemon fish.

D. Some sharks catch small fish but like the lemon fish.

In Your Own Words

5. Combine these groups of words into one sentence.

Sharks have many teeth. Sharks' teeth are sharp. Sharks' teeth are set in rows.

5.
Are there words that are repeated in each sentence?

Editing

Once a hungry traveler had an idea. He picked up a rock and put it in his pocket. Then he walked to a nearby village and put his plan into action. There he made a fire, filled a pot with water, and tossed in the rock.

A curious villager approached. "What are you doing?" she asked.

"I am making stone soup," the traveler replied. "I'll gladly share some with you. I just wish I had some potatoes." After hesitating. The villager offered to get some.

The villager returned with the potatoes and added them to the pot. Then her friend came over. "What are you doing?" the friend asked.

"We are making stone soup," the first villager replied.

"I'll share it with you," said the traveler. "I just wish it had some tomatoes. Then it would be perfect." The friend. Offered to share a few tomatoes.

Soon the whole village was gathered around the pot. People offered to share beans, carrots, and ham. The traveler stirred the soup, and a wonderful aroma filled the air. When the soup was ready, he dished out soup for himself and for the villagers. Everyone loved the delicious soup. Everyone begged the traveler to leave his magic soup stone. The traveler smiled to himself, and he tossed the stone to the first villager. As he headed out of town, he tucked another rock in his pocket.

---

1. Which sentence from the passage is a sentence fragment?

   A. The villager returned with the potatoes and added them to the pot.

   B. Offered to share a few tomatoes.

   C. "What are you doing?" she asked.

   D. I just wish it had some tomatoes.

2. Which sentence from the passage is a compound sentence?

   A. The traveler smiled to himself, and he tossed the stone to the first villager.

   B. As he headed out of town, he tucked another rock in his pocket.

   C. People offered to share beans, carrots, and ham.

   D. Everyone loved the delicious soup.

3. Which sentence from the passage is a simple sentence?

   A. Once a hungry traveler had an idea.

   B. He picked up a rock and put it in his pocket.

   C. Then he walked to a nearby village and put his plan into action.

   D. There he made a fire, filled a pot with water, and tossed in the rock.

4. Which of the following is **not** a complete sentence?

   A. A curious villager approached.

   B. "What are you doing," she asked.

   C. After hesitating.

   D. The villager offered to get some.

5. Which sentence from the passage is a compound sentence?

   A. "I am making stone soup," the traveler replied.

   B. Soon the whole village was gathered around the pot.

   C. The traveler stirred the soup, and a wonderful aroma filled the air.

   D. He dished out soup for himself and for the villagers.

6. Which is the **best** way to combine the following sentences?

   Everyone loved the delicious soup.
   Everyone begged the traveler to
   leave his magic soup stone.

   A. Everyone loved the soup, while they begged the traveler to leave his stone.

   B. Everyone loved the soup, everyone begged the traveler to leave his stone.

   C. Everyone loved the soup and they begged the traveler to leave his stone.

   D. Everyone loved the soup, and they begged the traveler to leave his stone.

Write It Out Read the following sentence. Break it up into smaller sentences to make the text easier to understand.

7. As he headed to the next village, the traveler held tightly to his rock and thought about how easily he had tricked the villagers, wondering if his plan would work in the next village, or if he would need to come up with some other way of getting food.

_____

_____

_____

Editing

WORDS TO KNOW   **Subject-verb agreement**   the use of a singular verb for a singular subject, and a plural verb for a plural subject

---

Read this sentence. Use the Hint to help you decide whether the subject and the verb agree.

Everyone is excited about the field trip to the symphony.

> **Hint**   The subject, *everyone*, is singular. The verb must agree with it. The verb in this sentence, *is*, is singular.

Try It!   Read this passage. As you read, circle the subject and <u>underline</u> the verb in each sentence.

(1)   Everyone in our class is excited today. Our class are planning our spring program. There has been a lot of discussion. This afternoon we will vote. Some students want to put on a play. *The Detective Chronicles* are one of our favorites. It would be an easy show to put on. One student wants to do a comedy show with jokes and skits. They are all great ideas.

(2)   Mrs. Dawson helps us list all of the ideas on the board. Next to each idea, we write the pros and cons. The pros are the good things about the idea. Then we each writes our favorite idea on a scrap of paper. Mrs. Dawson collects the votes and place a check mark next to each choice. I think this is fair. Now, I just have to decide!

Now, use the passage to answer the questions on the following page.

1. Which sentence contains an error in subject-verb agreement?

   A. Everyone in our class is excited today.

   B. Our class are planning our spring program.

   C. This afternoon we will vote.

   D. Some students want to put on a play.

2. Which sentence contains an error in subject-verb agreement?

   A. *The Detective Chronicles* are one of our favorites.

   B. It would be an easy show to put on.

   C. One student wants to do a comedy show with jokes and skits.

   D. They are all great ideas.

2.

A play is a piece of work with a title. Is it singular or plural?

3. Which sentence from the passage is **not** written correctly?

   A. Mrs. Dawson helps us list all of the ideas on the board.

   B. Next to each idea, we write the pros and cons.

   C. The pros are the good things about the idea.

   D. Then we each writes our favorite idea on a scrap of paper.

4. Which sentence from the passage is **not** written correctly?

   A. Mrs. Dawson collects the votes and place a check mark next to each choice.

   B. I think this is fair.

   C. Now, I just have to decide!

   D. There has been a lot of discussion.

4.

Does the noun, *Mrs. Dawson*, agree with both verbs?

In Your Own Words

5. Rewrite the following sentence, correcting any errors.

   The price of tickets are the next thing we have to agree on.

5.

Think carefully about the subject of this sentence. is the subject singular or plural?

_____

_____

Editing

Yearbook Committee Report

Class Pages: Each of the pages are being looked at carefully to make sure all the names are spelled correctly. Beth and Cameron noticed that the wrong name was under Mr. Gomez's picture. Neither Mrs. Helmer's nor Ms. Williams's page is done. We hope to have them finished on Wednesday.

Sports: Vinegar and oil dressing are not good for pages! Someone spilled salad dressing on the sports page. We are redoing that page. It will be done tomorrow.

Activities: We are working on the school-play page. *Two Brave Soldiers* are the title of the play. We will use pictures of flags and banners on the page. Megan and Tia are taking a few more pictures for this section.

Cover Design: We are having a contest to name the book. So far, *Silverlake Special* is in the lead. *Silverlake Stars* are in second place. The contest to name the yearbook ends on Thursday.

Sales: The price last year was $10. We are increasing the price by $2. Twelve dollars are not too much for a yearbook. We will begin our sales drive in March.

Advertising: All students needs to help with our advertising. We ask that each person contact two businesses to see if they will sponsor an ad. Several ads have already been sold. Eli and Molly are in charge of designing the ads.

---

1. Which sentence from the passage contains an error in subject–verb agreement?

   A. Each of the pages are being looked at carefully to make sure all the names are spelled correctly.

   B. Beth and Cameron noticed that the wrong name was under Mr. Gomez's picture.

   C. Neither Mrs. Helmer's nor Ms. Williams's page is done.

   D. We hope to have them finished on Wednesday.

2. Which sentence from the passage contains an error in subject–verb agreement?

   A. Vinegar and oil dressing are not good for pages!

   B. Someone spilled salad dressing on the sports page.

   C. We are redoing that page.

   D. It will be done tomorrow.

3. Which sentence from the passage is **not** written correctly?

    A. We are working on the school-play page.

    B. *Two Brave Soldiers* are the title of the play.

    C. We will use pictures of flags and banners on the page.

    D. Megan and Tia are taking a few more pictures for this section.

4. Which sentence from the passage contains an error in subject-verb agreement?

    A. We are having a contest to name the book.

    B. So far, *Silverlake Special* is in the lead.

    C. *Silverlake Stars* are in second place.

    D. The contest to name the yearbook ends on Thursday.

5. Which sentence from the passage contains an error in subject-verb agreement?

    A. The price last year was $10.

    B. We are increasing the price by $2.

    C. Twelve dollars are not too much for a yearbook.

    D. We will begin our sales drive in March.

6. Which sentence from the passage is not written correctly?

    A. All students needs to help with our advertising.

    B. We ask that each person contact two businesses to see if they will sponsor and ad.

    C. Several ads have already been sold.

    D. Eli and Molly are in charge of designing the ads.

Write It Out Rewrite these sentences in the space below, correcting any errors.

7. Get your yearbook today! *Silverake Stars* are on sale in the library. Twelve dollars are all it costs.

    _____

    _____

    _____

    _____

Punctuation: The Comma

WORDS TO KNOW **Comma** a mark of punctuation that shows a pause, connects ideas, or separates items in a list

 **Review It!** Read this sentence. Use the Hint to help you decide if the comma is used correctly.

When the game was over, we all went to a restaurant for pizza.

> **Hint** Where do you naturally pause when you read the sentence? That's where the comma belongs.

 **Try It!** Read this passage. As you read, notice how commas are used—and where they are missing.

(1)   Have you ever noticed the raised bumps by the numbers on an elevator? These are Braille letters. The bumps are raised so that blind people can read them with their fingers. They were invented by Louis Braille.

(2)   As a boy, Louis got an eye infection that made him blind. He received a scholarship to a school for the blind. The school used special books. The words were not printed flat on the pages. Instead, the letters were raised. He tried to read them but it was hard to tell the letters apart.

(3)   When Louis was 12 years old, he decided to find a better way. He gave it some thought and he came up with new system. His system had six raised dots arranged in patterns to represent different letters. Now it was easier to tell the letters apart. Many blind people who could not write could now use Braille. They could write using a stylus and paper to make the dots. Braille provided a way for blind people to write read and learn.

Now, use the passage to answer the questions on the following page.

1. Choose the sentence that has the correct punctuation.

   A. As a boy, Louis got an eye infection that made him blind.

   B. As a boy Louis got an eye infection that made him blind.

   C. As a boy Louis, got an eye infection, that made him blind.

   D. As a boy Louis got an eye infection, it made him blind.

2. Choose the sentence that has the correct punctuation.

   A. He tried to read them but, it was hard to tell the letters apart.

   B. He tried to read them but it was hard to tell the letters apart.

   C. He tried to read them but, it was hard, to tell the letters apart.

   D. He tried to read them, but it was hard to tell the letters apart.

   > **2.**
   > Where do you hear a pause when you read this sentence?

3. Which sentence is punctuated correctly?

   A. He gave it some thought and, he came up with a new system.

   B. He gave it some thought and he came up, with a new system.

   C. He gave it some thought, and he came up with a new system.

   D. He gave it, some thought, and he came up with a new system.

4. Which sentence is punctuated correctly?

   A. Braille provided a way for blind people to write, read, and learn.

   B. Braille provided a way, for blind people to write read and learn.

   C. Braille provided a way for blind people, to write read, and learn.

   D. Braille provided a way for blind people to write read and learn.

   > **4.**
   > In a sentence that ends with a list of three items, how are commas used to separate them?

In Your Own Words

5. Rewrite the following sentence, correcting any errors.

   Louis Braille was a young child but he was able to help many people.

   _____

   _____

   > **5.**
   > This sentence contains two separate ideas. How do you show a break between them?

Editing

Read this passage. Answer the questions that follow it.

Today I say good-bye to Champ, the puppy I have been taking care of for the past year. It's a little sad but I know it is the right thing. Our family raises puppies to be used as guide dogs for the blind.

The guide dogs are trained to walk in a straight line unless they see an obstacle. They will stop at curbs and they will alert the person they are guiding. They can even find common places such as bus stops for their owner.

We teach the puppies to obey commands. We take the puppies everywhere with us, even to the grocery store. This helps them get used to being around people. It would be dangerous for a guide dog to run off when they are leading a person. The dogs work but we also play with them. The truth is Champ could chase a tennis ball for hours!

Most of our dogs go to guide school, but some others help community groups. Champ has learned to obey and he is ready to go to guide school. There he will learn to wear a special harness lead a person and watch for danger. I'm sad to say good-bye to Champ, but we know he will be happy. He will make a difference. And soon we will get our next puppy, Lucy.

---

1. Choose the sentence that has the correct punctuation.

A. It's a little sad but I know it is the right thing.

B. It's a little sad, but I know it is the right thing.

C. It's a little sad but, I know it is the right thing.

D. It's a little sad, but, I know it is the right thing.

2. Choose the sentence that has the correct punctuation.

A. They will stop at curbs and they will alert the person they are guiding.

B. They will stop at curbs, and, they will alert the person they are guiding.

C. They will stop at curbs and, they will alert the person they are guiding.

D. They will stop at curbs, and they will alert the person they are guiding.

3. Which sentence is written correctly?

   A. The dogs work, but we also play with them.

   B. The dogs work but, we also play with them.

   C. The dogs work, but, we also play with them.

   D. The dogs work but we also play with them.

4. Where should commas be added in this sentence?

   There he will learn to wear a special harness lead a person and watch for danger.

   A. There he will learn, to wear a special harness, lead a person and watch for danger.

   B. There he will learn to wear, a special harness, lead a person and watch, for danger.

   C. There he will learn to wear a special harness lead a person, and watch for danger.

   D. There he will learn to wear a special harness, lead a person, and watch for danger.

5. Which sentence is punctuated correctly?

   A. Champ has learned to obey, and, he is ready to go to guide school.

   B. Champ has learned to obey and he is ready to go to guide school.

   C. Champ has learned to obey, and he is ready to go to guide school.

   D. Champ has learned to obey and, he is ready to go to guide school.

6. Which sentence is punctuated correctly?

   A. The truth is Champ could chase a tennis ball for hours!

   B. The truth is Champ could chase a tennis ball, for hours!

   C. The truth is, Champ could chase a tennis ball for hours!

   D. The truth is, Champ, could chase a tennis ball for hours!

Write It Out Rewrite the following sentence in the space below, correcting any errors.

7. Some puppies have a hard time learning to obey but most puppies learn quickly.

_____

_____

_____

WORDS TO KNOW   **Capitalization**   use of an uppercase letter to begin a sentence, a proper noun (United States, Charles, Jean), or a personal title (Dr., Mr.). Capitalization is also used in titles *(The Wizard of Oz)*, abbreviations (FBI, YMCA), and the pronoun "I."

Review It!   Read this sentence. Use the Hint to help you understand how capitalization is used in the sentence.

We will visit the Grand Canyon this summer.

> **Hint**   The word *We* is capitalized because it begins the sentence. *Grand Canyon* is capitalized because it is a proper noun that names a specific geographical place.

Try It!   Read this passage. As you read, watch for errors in capitalization.

(1)   Weddell seals are named after mr. james weddell, an explorer. They live in Antarctica, farther south than any other seal. They live about 800 miles from the south pole. Other animals of Antarctica migrate, but Weddell seals do not. They are able to survive the freezing cold Winters. They have a thick layer of fat that helps them stay warm. They also have short, dense fur that acts like a jacket.

(2)   Weddell seals are great hunters. They can dive to Amazing Depths in search of fish, squid, and other small animals. They are able to close their nostrils and hold their breath for up to an hour, which also helps them to catch their prey. Weddell seals spend a great deal of time underwater. This helps keep them fairly safe from predators such as leopard seals and killer whales, which must breathe air more often.

Now, use the passage to answer the questions on the following page.

Editing

1. Which of the following has correct capitalization?

   A. Weddell seals are named after mr. James Weddell, an explorer.

   B. Weddell seals are named after mr. James Weddell, an Explorer.

   C. Weddell seals are named after Mr. James Weddell, an explorer.

   D. Weddell seals are named after Mr. James Weddell, an Explorer.

2. Which of the following has correct capitalization?

   A. They live about 800 Miles from the south pole.

   B. They live about 800 miles from the south Pole.

   C. They live about 800 miles from the South pole.

   D. They live about 800 miles from the South Pole.

   2.
   Is there a proper noun that needs to be capitalized?

3. Which sentence has a capitalization error?

   A. Other animals of Antarctica migrate, but Weddell seals do not.

   B. They are able to survive the freezing cold Winters.

   C. They have a thick layer of fat that helps them stay warm.

   D. They also have short, dense fur that acts like a jacket.

4. Which sentence has a capitalization error?

   A. They can dive to Amazing Depths in search of fish, squid, and other small animals.

   B. Weddell seals spend a great deal of time underwater.

   C. This helps keep them fairly safe from predators such as leopard seals and killer whales.

   D. They are able to close their nostrils and hold their breath for up to an hour.

   4.
   Is something capitalized that shouldn't be?

In Your Own Words

5. Rewrite the sentences using the correct capitalization.

   my dad and dr. wells work together at nasa. they use satellites to study the migration of whales.

   _____

   _____

   5.
   Which words are proper nouns? Are there any abbreviations that should be capitalized?

Editing

My name is buniq, which means "sweet daughter" in the inuit language. Some people call inuit people eskimos, but i just call them family. We live in the southern part of alaska on the alaska peninsula. I love being an Inuit.

We are known for our artwork, especially our beautiful stone carvings. I love walking through the village and seeing everyone's creations. Mr. James Houston visited our village in the 1940s and taught my people the art of printmaking. Some people in our village sell their art to people all around the world. Many of the artists in our village make nature prints. People think Alaska is bare and covered with snow all the time. However, in the spring, the fields are filled with tiny wildflowers. Even winter provides inspiration, with icicles hanging from pines, and hares leaving paw prints as they leap across the snow

I am also an artist. I work with my Mother, whose name is Nukka. She makes beautiful nature prints. I write poems to go with them. We recently published a book called *a walk with the inuit*. I am planning a trip to a museum in albany, new york, to share my book at an exhibit of Inuit art.

1. Which sentence has correct capitalization?

   A. My name is Buniq, which means "sweet daughter" in the Inuit language.

   B. My name is buniq, which means "Sweet Daughter" in the inuit language.

   C. My name is buniq, which means "Sweet Daughter" in the Inuit Language.

   D. My name is Buniq, which means "sweet daughter" in the inuit language.

2. Which sentence has correct capitalization?

   A. Some people call inuit people Eskimos, but i just call them family.

   B. Some People call inuit people eskimos, but I just call them family.

   C. Some people call Inuit people Eskimos, but I just call them family.

   D. Some people call Iniut People Eskimos, but I just call them Family.

3. Which sentence has correct capitalization?

   A. We live in the southern part of alaska on the alaska peninsula.

   B. We live in the southern part of Alaska on the Alaska Peninsula.

   C. We live in the Southern part of Alaska on the Alaska peninsula.

   D. We live in the Southern part of Alaska on the Alaska Peninsula.

4. Which sentence has correct capitalization?

   A. We recently published a book called *a walk with the inuit.*

   B. We recently published a book called *A walk with the inuit.*

   C. We recently published a book called *A Walk With The Inuit.*

   D. We recently published a book called *A Walk with the Inuit.*

5. Which sentence contains a capitalization error?

   A. She makes beautiful nature prints.

   B. I wrote poems to go with them.

   C. However, in the spring, the fields are filled with tiny wildflowers.

   D. I work with my Mother, whose name is Nukka.

6. Which sentence contains a capitalization error?

   A. Some people in our village sell their art to people all around the world.

   B. I love walking through the village and seeing everyone's creations.

   C. I am planning a trip to a museum in albany, new york, to share my book at an exhibit of Inuit art.

   D. We are known for our artwork, especially our beautiful stone carvings.

Write It Out Rewrite the following sentence, correcting any errors in capitalization.

7. in january, i read a book called <u>alaska: the great outdoors.</u>

_____

_____

Editing

| WORDS TO KNOW | **Spelling** the standard or correct pattern of letters to make a word |

Review It! Read these sentences. Use the Hint to help you determine whether all the words are spelled correctly.

I went to the shelter to choose a puppy.
I couldn't decide on one because all of
the puppies were so cute.

Hint Look at the words *puppy* and *puppies*. Which letters were dropped and which were added to make the plural form of the word?

Try It! Read this passage. As you read, underline any the words that are spelled incorrectly.

(1) Princess Pat loved everything about horses. Most ladys rode their horses slowly and gracefully. But not Princess Pat. She liked to take off at a gallop.

(2) One day, Princess Pat took out her mare, Dasher, for a long run. She closed her eyes, feeling the wind on her face. She didn't see the foxs, but Dasher did. Dasher nieghed loudly and reared back. Princess Pat fell to the ground.

(3) When Princess Pat got up, she saw that Dasher's front leg was hurt. "Hopefully, she will be fine," thought Princess Pat. She crossed her fingers. "Oh, I would give all my wishs just to have her be okay." Luckily, Pat's brother rode by. He made sure that Pat was okay. Then he wrapped Dasher's leg with his scarf. They slowly led the horse home. Dr. Randall examined Dasher carefuly. Princess Pat was releived to hear that Dasher would be fine.

Now, use the passage to answer the questions on the following page.

1. Which sentence has a spelling error?

   A. Princess Pat loved everything about horses.

   B. Most ladys rode their horses slowly and gracefully.

   C. She liked to take off at a gallop.

   D. When Princess Pat got up, she saw that Dasher's front leg was hurt.

2. Which sentence has a spelling error?

   A. One day, Princess Pat took out her mare, Dasher, for a long run.

   B. Princess Pat closed her eyes, feeling the wind on her face.

   C. She didn't see the foxs, but Dasher did.

   D. He made sure that Pat was okay.

2.
What ending is added to pluralize a noun ending in -x?

3. Which sentence has a spelling error?

   A. Dasher nieghed loudly and reared back.

   B. Princess Pat fell to the ground.

   C. They slowly led the horse home.

   D. "Hopefully, she will be fine," thought Princess Pat.

3.
Is *ei* or *ie* generally used in words with a long *a* sound?

4. Which sentence has a spelling error?

   A. She crossed her fingers.

   B. "Oh, I would give all my wishs for her to be okay."

   C. Luckily, Pat's brother rode by.

   D. He wrapped Dasher's leg with his scarf.

In Your Own Words

5. Rewrite the sentences below, correcting the spelling errors.

   Dr. Randall examined Dasher carefuly. Princess Pat was releived to hear that Dasher would be fine.

   _____

   _____

5.
Look at each word closely. Which ones do not follow basic spelling rules?

Editing

Read this passage. Answer the questions that follow it.

Tom's room had three bookshelfs. They were filled with many of the things you would find in any ten-year-old boy's room. Tom had books, baseballs, and model cars. Tom also had several trophys for soccer, tennis, and football. What he didn't have was a trophy for the most home runs. Tom wanted that trophy badly.

Each day after school, he went to the bating cage to practice. He hit ball after ball forcefully. Now, here he was in the final game of the season. Tom just needed to hit one home run to beat the record. At his first turn at bat, Tom marched to the plate with a look of determination. He thought he saw the perfect pitch. "Wait for it!" he coached himself. As it zoomed toward the plate, Tom kept his eyes on the ball. He controled his movements, making contact.

The ball went high and straight into the outfield. "Please, don't catch it!" he hopped as he rounded the bases. As Tom headed for home, the second-base player wound up to throw the ball to the catcher. Tom ran faster than he thought he could. His heart was pounding in his chest. He slid onto the plate as the umpire yelled, "Safe!" Tom had finally acheived his goal.

1. **Which sentence has a spelling error?**

   A. Tom's room had three bookshelfs.

   B. They were filled with the same things you would find in any ten-year-old boy's room.

   C. What he didn't have was a trophy for most home runs.

   D. Tom wanted that trophy badly.

2. **Which sentence has a spelling error?**

   A. The ball went high and straight into the outfield.

   B. Tom just needed to hit one home run to beat the record.

   C. At his first turn at bat, Tom marched to the plate with determination.

   D. Tom also had several trophys for soccer, tennis, and football.

3. **Which sentence has a spelling error?**

   A. He thought he saw the perfect pitch.

   B. Each day after school, he went to the bating cage to practice.

   C. "Wait for it!" he coached himself.

   D. As the pitch zoomed toward the plate, Tom kept his eyes on the ball.

4. **Which sentence has a spelling error?**

   A. "Please, don't catch it!" he hopped as he rounded the bases.

   B. Now, here he was in the final game of the season.

   C. Tom ran faster than he thought he could.

   D. He slid onto the plate as the umpire yelled, "Safe!"

5. **Which phrase has a spelling error?**

   A. Each day after school

   B. controled his movements

   C. As Tom headed for home

   D. the second-base player wound up

6. **Which phrase has a spelling error?**

   A. to throw the ball to the catcher

   B. ran faster than he thought

   C. His heart was pounding

   D. acheived his goal

Write It Out Rewrite the sentence below, correcting the spelling errors.

7. To be strong hiters, many baseball players lift wieghts.

_____

_____

Editing

Words to Know

 argument the writer's position on a topic, including how the writer feels about the topic and reasons why **(Page 38)**

 capitalization use of an uppercase letter to begin a sentence, a proper noun, a personal title, a title of a book or article, an abbreviation, and the pronoun "I" **(Page 114)**

cause the reason why something happens **(Page 50)**

characters the people or animals about whom a story is told **(Page 74)**

comma a mark of punctuation that shows a pause, connects ideas, or separates items in a list **(Page 110)**

compare to show how things are alike, or similar **(Page 54)**

compound sentence two or more simple sentences put together **(Page 102)**

conclusion an overall opinion that you form after reading a passage. A conclusion is based on what you've read but is not stated directly in the passage. **(Page 26)**

context clues the words, phrases, or sentences around or near an unfamiliar word that help you understand its meaning **(Page 6)**

contrast to show how things are different **(Page 54)**

 drama a form of writing that is divided into acts and scenes, and has dialogue and stage directions **(Page 62)**

 effect something that happens as a result of the cause **(Page 50)**

essential information information that is connected directly to the topic of the passage **(Page 34)**

 fact a statement that can be proven to be true **(Page 30)**

fiction any story about imaginary people and events **(Page 62)**

format how text is arranged and organized. Features such as the table of contents, headings, glossary, and index help the reader understand the organization of a text and the information it contains. **(Page 46)**

 graphic organizers visual aids that show information in an easy-to-read way. Tables, timelines, and bar graphs are examples. **(Page 18)**

 inference an educated guess based on what you are reading. When you make an inference, you are figuring out something the writer has not stated directly. **(Page 22)**

main idea the most important idea of a passage, or what the passage is mostly about (Page 10)

metaphor a direct comparison of two things without using the words *like* or *as* (Page 90)

nonessential information information that is not important to the topic of the passage (Page 34)

opinion a statement of personal feeling or belief (Page 30)

personification giving human qualities to something that is not human, like an animal or an object (Page 94)

plot the series of events that take place in a story. Plot consists of a conflict, a climax, and a resolution. (Page 66)

poetry a form of writing that has stanzas and lines that may rhyme (Page 62)

research finding information for a certain purpose (Page 42)

rhyme when words end with the same sound (Page 82)

rhythm the use of stressed and unstressed syllables to create a beat (Page 82)

sentence fragment an incomplete sentence. A sentence fragment is missing a subject or a predicate. (Page 102)

sequence the order in which events happen in an informational passage or a story (Page 58)

setting where and when a story takes place (Page 70)

simile a comparison of two unlike things using the words *like* or *as* (Page 86)

simple sentence a group of words that has one subject and one predicate (Page 102)

sources books, encyclopedias, articles, and websites that contain information about the topic you are researching (Page 42)

subject-verb agreement the use of a singular verb for a singular subject, and a plural verb for a plural subject (Page 106)

supporting details the information that supports, or backs up, the main idea (Page 14)

symbolism a literary device that uses an object to represent a theme, idea, or emotion (Page 98)

theme the central idea of a story; a lesson about life (Page 78)

My Words